Praise for *The Turnkey Revolution*

"I'm a longtime admirer of Chris Clothier and Memphis Invest. This book is more evidence that Chris and his team not only understand real estate, but, more importantly, understand the needs and concerns of the real estate investor. Chris Clothier gives real estate investors a clear and dependable path to financial success. This book is not only useful and informative, it's a pleasure to read. If there's one thing that today's investor wants, it's peace of mind. Chris Clothier's turnkey real estate plan instills confidence with rock solid advice that makes sense."

—JOE CALLOWAY, AUTHOR, *BE THE BEST AT WHAT MATTERS MOST*

"Read this book! The road map and resources shared in *The Turnkey Revolution* empowered me to do what I have always wanted to do: own a bunch of real estate headache free. Turnkey investing, the Clothier way, allows you to analyze, buy, and benefit from buy-and-hold real estate without dealing with the potatoes stuck in the toilets. Chris offers a straightforward, illuminating education for any investor or would-be investor who wants to leverage real estate and its benefits without pitfalls. This book lets me master, buy, and hold real estate, leveraging the best education and professionals in the business."

—PAUL ESAJIAN, COFOUNDER AND OWNER OF FORTUNEBUILDERS, INC.

the TURNKEY REVOLUTION

the TURNKEY REVOLUTION

HOW TO PASSIVELY BUILD YOUR REAL ESTATE PORTFOLIO FOR MORE INCOME, FREEDOM, AND PEACE OF MIND

CHRISTOPHER D. CLOTHIER

New York Chicago San Francisco Athens London Madrid
Mexico City Milan New Delhi Singapore Sydney Toronto

1 2 3 4 5 6 7 8 9   QFR   23 22 21 20 19 18

ISBN   978-1-260-11753-0
MHID   1-260-11753-7

e-ISBN   978-1-260-11754-7
e-MHID   1-260-11754-5

This publication is designed to provide accurate and authoritative information in regard to the subject matter covered. It is sold with the understanding that neither the author nor the publisher is engaged in rendering legal, accounting, securities trading, or other professional services. If legal advice or other expert assistance is required, the services of a competent professional person should be sought.

 —From a Declaration of Principles Jointly Adopted by a Committee of the American Bar Association and a Committee of Publishers and Associations

Library of Congress Cataloging-in-Publication Data

Names: Clothier, Christopher, author.
Title: The turnkey revolution : how to passively build your real estate portfolio
 for more income, freedom, and peace of mind / Christopher Clothier.
Description: New York : McGraw-Hill, [2018]
Identifiers: LCCN 2017053674| ISBN 9781260117530 (alk. paper) | ISBN
 1260117537
Subjects: LCSH: Real estate investment. | Portfolio management.
Classification: LCC HD1382.5 .C56 2018 | DDC 332.63/24--dc23 LC record
 available at https://lccn.loc.gov/2017053674

//

This book is dedicated to my wife, Michelle; my sons, Grayson and Grant; my daughters, Sophie, Margo, and Andi Rose; my family, especially my mom, who always believed I would write a book; and the entire team here at Memphis Invest, especially my partners, my dad, Kent Clothier, Sr., and my younger brother, Brett, for putting up with me on a daily basis!

//

CONTENTS

ACKNOWLEDGMENTS

I could never have undertaken writing a book like this without the support and love of my wife Michelle and my five kids, Grayson, Grant, Sophie, Margo, and Andi Rose. Their constant love and encouragement has made this dream of publishing a book a dream worth fighting for.

I also owe a huge debt of gratitude to my dad, Kent Clothier Sr., and my two brothers, Brett Clothier and Kent Clothier Jr. Much in the same way as Memphis Invest started out for my father as notes on a restaurant napkin, this book began in another form, as a collection of blog posts and notes that have grown over time into something much bigger than I ever could have imagined.

I also want to acknowledge the thousands—and I do mean thousands—of real estate investors I have had the privilege of meeting and speaking with over the last 10 years. Those conversations, some of which I recount here in this book, helped shape my ideas of what it means to serve others in business.

I hope each of you has found the courage to take the necessary steps toward finding success in real estate. Every conversation we've had, every email we've exchanged, and every question you've asked me on stage has led to this book. May the answers in these pages arm you with a clear sense of vision and help guide your journey on the path to a prosperous future.

Lastly, this book would never have happened without the encouragement and support of my friends and colleagues who encouraged me to follow my passion and educate from my pen. There are too many people to thank to name individually. Nonetheless, know that I am grateful for the role each of you has played in helping me find the courage to take this next step.

THE TURNKEY REVOLUTION BEGINS

I t was a Thursday night in the fall of 2003, and Kent Cloth-ier Sr. had just finished speaking at the monthly meeting of the Memphis Investors Group at the Home Builders Association building. It was a typical real estate investing group that met monthly, and they were constantly looking for speakers to share insights, stories, tips, and sometimes sell DIY programs.

He was invited to speak by the group for one reason. He was an action taker. He wasn't interested in hanging out for dough-nuts and coffee at the monthly meetings. In fact, a favorite saying of his in business was that "he didn't have time for the dough-nut eaters." He was interested in meeting who he needed to meet, learning what he needed to learn, and getting down to business.

It was a normal talk for him and an uneventful evening that was about to get turned upside down. After the meeting, he was approached by a small group of listeners who wanted to pick his brain on how they too could get started. Only this group had a very specific question. They were airline pilots at Federal Express there in Memphis and found themselves with-out knowledge and barely enough time to invest in real estate. What they did have was the means and desire to invest in real estate and a pretty good idea that owning long-term rental properties passively was a good way to grow the money they had and build additional income.

The question they had for him was, Would he help them build their portfolios? Would he help find properties for them, use his renovation connections and crews to fix the properties, and then hand them off to his property management team?

Kent Sr. spent the next few minutes asking them what they were looking for and exactly what they expected. He explained that he would want to make an income for putting in his time and expertise. He expected to make a profit for doing the work. They all agreed that they expected him to make a profit. After all, they said, "why would we want to go into business with someone who didn't want to make a profit?" They left the meeting that night agreeing to meet later in the week.

A few days later, on the back of a restaurant napkin, Kent Sr. laid out the blueprint for a new company. The blueprint for a company that would excel at finding great investment properties, renovating them to a high standard so they were in demand, and providing a new style of property management. A style focused on attracting and satisfying the needs of residents. A customer service company that would happen to be in the real estate investing business.

A restaurant napkin isn't quite big enough to hold a lot of details. But it was big enough to hold a revolutionary idea. Kent Clothier Sr. happens to be my dad, and he happened to be laying out the details of what would become *The Turnkey Revolution*.

A FOOT IN THE DOOR

Everyone is interested in real estate.

Our culture loves the idea of real estate investing. We devour stories about people who went from rags to riches flipping houses. We watch episode after episode of renovation reality shows on TV: a quick half hour from wreck to rental property.

Real estate investing is glamorous. Real estate investing is easy to talk about. But it's more complicated than it looks.

The deeper you go into real estate, the uglier it seems to get behind the scenes. Horror stories start to come out of the woodwork. You don't know what you don't know, and what you don't know loses you money. The reality of investing in real estate has little to do with the "reality" we see during the 30-minute snippets.

Even if you can afford to invest in real estate education, you still get blindsided by surprises. No amount of education or online message boards can educate an investor to what it is really like when you pull the trigger and actually own an investment property.

When you bring the rest of life into the picture, things get even more complex. You're not just investing in real estate for the heck of it. You have dreams you're working to fulfill. Maybe you're trying to save for your wedding or your kid's college education. Maybe you want to fund a comfortable retirement and leave a legacy for your family.

Often the investment dollars we use come from the money we've put aside to fulfil the dreams we have for our families. It may not be life or death, but it can sure feel like it when we put everything we have on the table. So, no, you are not just investing in real estate, you are investing in your very future.

Whatever the case, you see that real estate is the right vehicle to take you to your goals. But if you get it wrong, you stand to lose more than just money. You're holding your future in your hands, and that's intimidating—even overwhelming. At the same time, you hear stories over and over again about people who played the real estate game and won. You're frustrated, because that should be you. Instead, you're sitting on the sidelines with no idea where to start.

You know that real estate itself is a solid, sound investment, and you have a strong desire to get involved. But what you don't have is the knowledge to do it safely or the time to manage a nest of chaotic rental properties. You desire a better way forward—a better way forward in life. Yet life seems to be the one thing getting in the way. With all of the hustle and bustle of working, maybe raising a family or starting a new chapter in life, time and knowledge seem to be the hardest hurdles to overcome. You have the desire, but you need something more.

You need a way to get your foot in the door.

THE WAY IN

What if I told you that you could safely, passively invest in real estate without giving up your current job, and without spending thousands of dollars and hours on education? What if I told you that not only could you invest in real estate, but you could passively own the properties themselves. You wouldn't have to invest in pieces of properties or shares with a bunch of other real estate investors you don't even know. You could invest in real investment property and own the deed yourself.

That opportunity exists. It is absolutely real. You can invest in real estate in a hands-off way with a team of experts in your corner—service-oriented people who will handle the dirty work for you and help you achieve your goals. There's a name for this method of passive investing.

It's called turnkey real estate investing.

When done correctly, turnkey real estate shortens the learning curve and allows you to successfully invest in the real estate market using the resources and knowledge that you already have. Instead of waiting, learning, and losing thousands of dollars on mistakes, it gives you the chance to invest safely, right now. And when you take advantage of it, it brings your goals within reach.

With turnkey in your corner, you can have that extra $2,500 a month in disposable income that you need to retire comfortably.

You can afford your daughter's wedding. You can buy a piece of real estate and have it paid off by the time your children are ready to go to college; that house is their college education fund.

That kind of money may not be enough for you to retire on, but it can make a huge difference in how you retire. It can open up a world of choices for you on where you retire, how you retire, and when you retire. It can make a huge difference in the choices your children have when they are older. The generational impact a small portfolio generating a few thousand dollars a month can have is enormous.

Most of the time, it doesn't take millions of dollars to achieve your dreams. The reality is that you just need a little bit more. You need to take what you have and make it go a little further, and you need to do it safely.

Turnkey real estate is a way to make that happen.

MY ROAD TO REAL ESTATE

I've been investing in turnkey real estate since 2003, when I bought my first property by accident.

My wife, Michelle, and I had just moved to Colorado from Tennessee with our 11-month-old son, Grayson. Before we could buy a home of our own in Colorado, we had to wait for our house in Tennessee to sell—or so I thought at the time.

The Tennessee house spent a year on the market.

All those months, the three of us lived in a 300-square-foot hotel room. I had moved my family across the country for an opportunity that would eventually culminate in founding my first company. Little did I know that my home in Tennessee was going to sit on the market for over a year. So, what had started out as a little adventure living temporarily in a hotel room turned into a long-term adventure in creative usage of space. Very little space!

Living in a hotel for a year was as good as it could be: we got to know the maids really well, and they were wonderful to our family. But it was still a hotel. We never had any peace and quiet. We had to eat out all the time, which got old after about a week. The dryer at the laundromat left burn marks on our clothes. Everything you can imagine about the annoyances of hotel living we experienced. About the time our son started thinking every house had a fountain Coke machine and daily breakfast buffet, I decided I had to get us out of the hotel and into a home in Colorado.

I just didn't know how to do it.

As luck would have it, Michelle had a younger sister who lived back in Tennessee, and she needed Michelle's help for a couple of weeks with her new baby. While they were back in Tennessee helping, my late-night TV habits were about to pay off.

If you watch enough cable TV, you will eventually come across a late-night infomercial hawking a "how-to" for real estate investors. One of the mainstays on TV from the first decade of the twenty-first century was a man named Carleton Sheets. Late one night while Michelle and Gray were gone, I saw a Carleton Sheets infomercial on TV.

"Real estate investing has created more millionaires than any investment in history," it said. "You can get started today, in your spare time, with no prior experience. You don't need to quit your full-time job. Call the number on your screen right now!"

Under other circumstances, I probably wouldn't have given it a second thought. We all have this idea that only certain people buy things off the TV late at night, and I knew that the Carleton Sheets program wasn't going to be a miracle solution. But I did see it for what it was: a creative and inexpensive opportunity to move forward. What did I have to lose? I remember thinking that I was sitting on the edge of a bed in the middle of a hotel room without a clue about how I was going to get out. What did I have to lose?

I bought that program for four easy payments of $37.99, and it really did spark new ideas in me about what was possible. Hey, selling the Tennessee house isn't my only option, I realized. I can trade houses with someone whose property is worth less and create the atmosphere for me to buy the house I need here in Colorado, right now.

And that's exactly what I did. I found a couple who wanted to buy my Tennessee house but were having trouble selling their own smaller place two blocks from Rhodes College in the heart of Memphis. My property sat on land and was a long commute from the city. Their property was a perfect college house. Their property was half the price of mine, and if I could figure out a creative way to swing a deal, I might be able to qualify to buy two houses: one in Memphis as a rental and one in Colorado as my primary residence. I hadn't had a chance to read or listen to half of the Carleton Sheets program, but the half I listened to sparked an idea, and my Realtor thought I was nuts.

HOUSE SWAP

I called my Realtor on the phone and asked her to send me over the listing on their property. I wanted her to go take a look at the property, and she thought I was wanting to give them advice on what they needed to do to sell their property. I explained to her that if their property was in a good location and could get a strong rent, I thought I would offer to buy their property and free them up to buy mine. I thought we could swap houses!

She wasn't the only one who thought I was crazy. The other couple thought I was completely off my rocker, and Michelle had no idea what I was talking about. I called my mortgage broker and asked if I could qualify to buy two houses if my property in Memphis was a cash-flowing rental property. He ran the figures and gave me the green light.

I was able to purchase their property and free them up to purchase my property. I then rented the Rhodes College house out to students, hiring a friend I trusted to handle both the renovation and the property management for me. It may not have been the most ideal situation to get started as a real estate investor, but it got me in the game.

Finally, we were able to move out of the hotel—and suddenly, I was also a real estate investor. My son was just starting to get used to the daily maid service and the pool, but Michelle and I were ready to move on. Not only was control of the present back in my hands, but control of the future was, too. That first property was valued at $120,000 at the time, and it represented more than just an investment property to me. "That rental property is Grayson's college fund," I told my wife. "By the time he's 18, we will own it free and clear, and it will pay for his education."

That little house in Memphis was my first turnkey property. It is where I started my rise as a real estate investor and my drive to help other investors. I had a long way to go and a lot to learn, but I knew at that moment I was moving in a different direction.

The day before I was trying to figure out my next moves. Was I staying in Denver, or was I moving back to Tennessee and starting my business there? Now, I was firmly planting my feet in Denver and starting to build my business with a new attitude toward my future. Real estate investing had suddenly become a major part of my strategy . . . and it was only the beginning.

TURNKEY LEADERSHIP

I don't just talk about turnkey real estate. My family and I have years of experience investing in all kinds of real estate ventures. I watched my dad buy investment properties in the 1980s. My older brother owned several properties in the late 1990s. I even rented one of his places while I was in college at the University of Memphis. When I started out in turnkey, owning real estate was nothing new to me. What was new to me was owning an investment property halfway across the country!

As a real estate investor, I've seen great success, and I've been crushed from making bad decisions—mistakes that became invaluable knowledge. I want to be clear right here at the beginning, I have made miserably poor decisions as an investor and made nearly every mistake a passive real estate investor can make. I also made some excellent investment decisions and learned from my mistakes. Over time, I realized that I could use my experience to help others. I could prevent them from making the same bad decisions I had made, so that they could invest safely in turnkey real estate the first time.

In 2003, my father founded, arguably, the most respected turnkey investment company in the country: Memphis Invest (MemphisInvest.com). In 2007, my younger brother, who had just graduated from the University of Mississippi with a degree in real estate, joined my father to grow and expand the company. They began growing the company by hiring young, energetic, and eager team members who had very little knowledge or experience in real estate, but a strong desire to learn. They started building a turnkey powerhouse before real estate investors knew what it truly meant to invest in turnkey properties. One year later, I joined the company as a partner as the head of sales and marketing and set out to change that.

As of 2018, our company has branches in Memphis, Dallas, Houston, Oklahoma City, and Little Rock. We have over

4,800 properties under management valued at over $600 million, and our investors bring in over $40 million per year in rental income.

Memphis Invest was named small business of the year by the *Memphis Business Journal* in 2013. We've been one of the fastest-growing companies on the *Inc.* magazine list of the 500/5000 fastest growing private companies since 2012. In 2017, we placed four companies on the *Inc.* magazine list. Our business has been featured in several national publications, including the *New York Times*, the *Wall Street Journal*, *USA Today*, and *Money* magazine.

The investors who work with us stay with us. Less than 1 percent of the real estate investors who have chosen to invest with Memphis Invest have left to go elsewhere over the history of our company. Our clients understand what's happening with their investments at all times. They have a strong relationship with their turnkey partner, and that gives them the confidence to keep moving forward in the direction of their dreams.

You're next.

THE COURAGE TO TAKE ACTION

This book can and should be more than your foundation for turnkey real estate investing. It should also be your validation that you're covering all your bases. Read it cover to cover, but don't stop there. Highlight the specific, actionable items you can do to be successful as a passive real estate investor. Then refer back to them as you grow your portfolio, and ask yourself, "Am I taking the right steps here?"

Real estate is like any other kind of investment: it comes with a certain level of risk. But when you follow the guidelines I'm about to share with you, you can minimize those risks and move forward toward the life you want for yourself and the people you love.

Investing in turnkey takes diligence, and even more than that, it takes courage. When I bought my first turnkey property in Tennessee, I knew that the way I did it wasn't perfect. But the important thing was that I went from somebody thinking about investing in real estate to somebody who was actually doing it.

Unlike the doughnut eaters my dad had always railed against, I was taking action. I was moving forward instead of standing around and waiting. I had the courage to act, and it gave me and my family a future we didn't have before.

You have to be bold, be brave, and take the necessary risks to achieve your dreams. That does not mean you need to be risky. There is a big difference between taking risk and being risky. That is where this book comes into the picture. I truly want to share my story and my experience in order to help guide you to making great investment decisions. This is your invitation to go from wishing and waiting to putting some serious momentum behind your drive to build a real estate portfolio.

The turnkey revolution is a simple guide—a road map offering the questions, answers, and tools necessary to build a reliable and productive passive portfolio. With stories culled from my own experiences and my conversations with real estate investors over the years, I will guide you step-by-step through the process of developing a smart, safe turnkey investment strategy. You will have the tools and the knowledge necessary to build your own passive portfolio. You will learn each of the steps to:

- **Design your vision.** Your "why" that drives you to hit your investment goals.

- **Finance your turnkey portfolio.** The ins and outs of smart turnkey financial decision making.

- **Research investment markets.** Learn to pick the right cities based on the right metrics.

- **Choose your turnkey company.** A bad company can ruin a great investment.

- **Create an investment plan.** Design a plan that fulfills your specific vision.

- **Make your investment.** Nothing happens until you take action!

- **Follow up with your investments.** A passive investor is never passive about his or her investments.

- **Expand your vision.** As your life grows, your vision should grow, too.

Throughout the book, I offer helpful tips and strategies successful turnkey investors have used to build their portfolios. Each chapter concludes with our Turnkey Safely Checklist™ and what I call Turnkey Mastery Tips—questions you want to consider to help safely plan your journey and chart your progress along the way.

THE OPEN ROAD TO YOUR FUTURE

Investing in real estate isn't a small decision. But when you do it right, it's a smart one. Building the future of your dreams doesn't all have to be hard work. It doesn't all have to be about the daily grind. Some of it can be smart planning and strategic decision making. Turnkey investing is for those who want to take action today to create a more comfortable future and lasting legacy. This is what I call the turnkey revolution.

You can buy a house once every two years like clockwork, then look up one day in the future and see that you're a millionaire. Not because you won the lottery, but because you made some really good, smart decisions, and you now own a million dollars' worth of real estate.

I have had the pleasure of meeting and speaking with thousands of real estate investors across the country. There are no real secrets to being a successful real estate investor. It's pretty simple, in fact. Some of the best real estate investors I know are doctors, librarians, schoolteachers, police officers, lawyers, bankers, executives, moms. They are the best investors I know because they took action. They didn't wait for a better time, and they didn't drown their dreams in the promise that someday they would get started. They took action, and to this day they continue to take simple steps—steps that give them strength by researching markets and choosing great turnkey partners. They don't have deep, technical knowledge of real estate, but they have portfolios that give them something far more important. They have their freedom.

Anyone can invest in turnkey real estate. It's not difficult, and it's not the domain of the rich and famous. As long as you do certain things to protect yourself, you can invest literally anywhere in the world. The opportunity exists, and it has the power to open the door to the future you want.

When you safely and passively invest in real estate, the barriers in front of you disappear. The steps you need to take become clear and concrete. You're not stuck on the sidelines anymore. Now, you're on the open road that will take you where you want to go. Now, you're a real estate investor.

Now, you're part of the turnkey revolution.

THE TURNKEY SAFELY CHECKLIST

Getting Started

- What is my background in real estate?

- Have I bought my first home to live in?

- Have I bought my first investment property?

- Do I have friends or family who have invested in real estate?

- Do I have a local real estate investors club to attend?

TURNKEY MASTERY TIPS

How long a company has been in business is very important.

A company that came through the real estate market crash and survived shows you that it has good systems and processes in place. A company that started after the crash and was built during the recovery may not have the experience necessary to protect you if and when a market takes a downturn. Keep that in mind!

CHAPTER 1

WHAT IS TURNKEY INVESTING?

Mark was your typical, hardworking, Mr. Do-anything-and-everything-it-takes-to-get-ahead-and-stay-ahead kind of guy. He was not only a high-level airline captain, he also owned a media production company with his wife. When he wasn't flying huge airplanes, he was producing shows for reality television, publishing regional magazines, and helping organize exhibitor shows. Mark also had his sights set on early retirement. With that kind of schedule, who wouldn't be looking forward to retirement?

He knew that real estate investing was the way to make his dream happen. So, he did what a lot of people do: he bought and renovated four rental houses, and he managed them himself.

It didn't take long for Mark to realize he was in over his head.

As a pilot, he worked 12 days a month. He co-owned the production company with his wife, so he had help with that company. Mark figured that would give him plenty of time to manage his four properties on his off days. However, what he didn't know was how much work that would be. He did everything on his own from the beginning. He found the properties, which took hours of research online and even more time driving to look at each one. He handled repairs by hiring and overseeing the contractors. He showed each of the properties to prospective renters himself and then collected rents. When he absolutely couldn't do it himself, he paid top dollar to have someone come in and take care of the job for him as a one-off.

Mark knew he was being inefficient with his money. Worse, he was putting in 40 hours a week keeping up his rentals. Not only could he not retire under his current plan, even if the numbers allowed it, he would just be trading one full-time job for another. He was exhausted.

That's when he saw my father give a speech about turnkey at a home and garden show he and his wife were putting on in Memphis. And suddenly, he saw a way forward. I remember the talk vividly not so much for the content but for the setting. Apparently, a talk about real estate investing was not a big draw at a home and garden show. There were four people in the audience that day. Myself, my brother, Mark, and his wife. Fortunately for all of us, the one person who needed to hear that message most that day was one of the four!

Mark contacted our company a week later. "I want to buy properties with you," he said immediately. "Where do I start?"

We helped Mark restructure his portfolio. Because he was buying houses from us, we agreed to take over the management of the four rentals he already had. Instead of the 30-year mortgages he currently had on those properties, we advised him to put everything on very short payoff periods. We looked at his goals and figured out how many houses Mark needed to make them happen. He bought more turnkey investment properties based on those numbers.

Mark began working with us in 2009. In 2014, he sent us an email out of the blue.

"My wife and I sat down this morning, and I brought her up to speed on our rental houses," he wrote. "Currently we have 27 houses with your company, all rented. We're bringing in $18,900 a month in gross income. Fifteen of our houses are paid off, and we will own the others free and clear in another 23 months.

"I'm 44 years old, and I've already scheduled my retirement from the airline in five years. This would not have been possible without you and your turnkey team. Thank you!"

WHAT IS TURNKEY REAL ESTATE?

If you search the term "turnkey real estate," one of the things you will quickly notice is that it gets thrown around a lot online. But what does it really mean?

Turnkey real estate is a form of passive investing in which you buy a piece of real estate from a company, and that company manages your property for you. The team you work with finds, renovates, and maintains the house you invest in, rather than you doing it all yourself, like Mark did. You don't even need to visit the house before you buy it. You can purchase it sight unseen from a company you trust and let the company handle the rest.

The philosophy behind the turnkey revolution is simple: it gives regular people a chance to invest in real estate.

For years, people have been able to invest in the stock market on their own. If you are willing to put in the time learning the system, you can jump online, look at ratings, and figure out how to do it yourself. But what you could never do was buy real estate in the same simple way—especially real estate located halfway around the world. Turnkey takes everyday people who are working their butts off to have what they have—airline pilots, firefighters, schoolteachers, sanitary workers, office assistants, police officers, even stay-at-home moms—and gives them a solution for their future.

One of the big benefits of turnkey real estate investing is that you don't have to quit your day job. You don't have to spend all your waking hours painting, scrubbing, and collecting rents. There are no late-night phone calls about busted pipes and broken air conditioners or heaters. Those issues are all eliminated when you buy turnkey real estate investments the right way. All you have to do is transact a property through a dependable team, and the wheel starts turning on its own.

I will get to the specifics of each step throughout the book. The most important step for you to remember at this point is that you want to let a dependable team that you have vetted and trust do the hard work and heavy lifting.

This chapter will give you a brief rundown on how turnkey came about, answer your questions about whether this is a "real" form of real estate investing, and help you decide if turnkey is right for you.

OLD STORY, NEW NAME

Turnkey real estate investing has been around for decades. It just wasn't always called turnkey.

Back in the sixties and seventies, passive investing worked by word of mouth. Investors with deep pockets found out about it through their real estate clubs. It didn't have a catchy name. The conversation went along the lines of, "Hey, I know you can't buy a garage here in San Francisco for $50,000, but guess what? You can get a whole house for $35,000 out in Fort Wayne, Indiana. I have a property out there, and I can manage it for you. Do you want to buy it from me?"

That was how it started. But the term *turnkey investing* wasn't coined until around 2006, and the Clothier family was the first to go mainstream with the term as a business model. That is when the business finally became a hot mainstream topic thanks to the Internet.

Once the Internet got a hold of it, turnkey exploded. The word *turnkey* began to dominate the space. Promoters came into the picture—companies that offered to funnel investors to property management businesses in exchange for a referral fee—and from then on, turnkey became a fixture in the bigger real estate picture.

But the downside of turnkey's fast rise to fame is that it hasn't been mainstream long enough to have clear standards. Every single week, somebody new raises a hand and says, "Hey, I have a turnkey property over here." That person might sell you a house, tell you that XYZ Company is going to manage it for you, and then disappear completely. Six months later, XYZ Company disappears, too, and you're stuck with a property on the other side of the country that you can't handle.

As for the promotional companies, that downside has just as big a bite. They bill themselves as a one-stop shop that handles all the due diligence for interested investors. They will vet the turnkey companies for you and take a fee for every transaction. Unfortunately, if a turnkey company is willing to pay a promoter's price, it can usually get business funneled its way. Let's just say that standards are sorely lacking in this area of the business as well. Rather than looking for the best in class, these promotional companies often promote anyone and everyone so long as they are willing to meet the price.

Scenarios like these have given turnkey a bad rap as a marketing term. The real estate world has its guard up and for good reason. But is it really as bad as some of the critics make it out to be?

THE TRUTH ABOUT TURNKEY

The main argument against turnkey investing is that the only people making money on it are the people selling the houses.

Most of the people who feel this way are active real estate investors. They believe that if you want to get involved with real estate at all, you need to do everything yourself: find the house, fix it up and paint the walls, and then maintain it on your own—just like Mark tried to do when he was starting out. Anything less, and they don't consider you a real investor.

If you ask these active investors how to invest in turnkey, their answer is, "You don't. You're a fool if you do. Go buy houses in your own city and learn this business on your own."

But the truth is that when you follow the right steps, turnkey will give you a safe, high-quality investment that will pay off year after year. Your income will be steady, and your reputable turnkey company will keep you abreast of what's going on with your property monthly.

It may look like you pay more for a property using the turnkey method than you do if you handle everything yourself. But what you're buying with those extra dollars is experience. You're not going to lose thousands of dollars on mistakes like active investors do. Instead, you're putting that money toward getting it right the first time, which actually saves you money in the end.

Not only are you a "real" real estate investor when you invest in turnkey, but you're an extremely intelligent real estate investor. This does not have to be an either/or scenario. It can absolutely be a scenario where you do both. You can actively invest in real estate and at the same time earn money on passive investments. Either way, when you decide to invest passively in turnkey, you are a "real" investor.

You've analyzed yourself and said, "I want to invest in real estate, but I don't have the knowledge or the time to do it myself. So, I'm going to surround myself with people who do have that knowledge and time. I'm going to own as much real estate as the next guy, and while he's out finding new tenants and repairing toilets, I'm going to collect my check."

You're still investing in real estate. You're just doing it the smart way for you.

IS TURNKEY RIGHT FOR YOU?

Now you understand what turnkey is and how it works. But real estate investing is a risk no matter what, and you still need to decide if turnkey investing is the right calculated risk for you. You simply need to ask yourself these questions to determine whether turnkey investing is the path you really want to be on.

Do I want to be hands-on or hands-off with my investments?

Turnkey real estate investing is not a hands-on experience at the day-to-day management level. You make your investment, and your turnkey company takes care of everything else. If you're the type of person who wants to be there every step of the way, choosing what color to paint the bedroom and which flowers to plant by the mailbox, you're going to be happier as a do-it-yourself style investor. Turnkey is a better fit for you if you are more of a find-the-best, invest-and-forget style of investor.

At the same time, turnkey is hands-on when it comes to managing your investment portfolio. You need to communicate with your turnkey partner and keep track of your monthly statements. If you're willing to do those things, but don't care about the physical details of owning an investment property, you'll enjoy the turnkey experience.

Do I want a quick return, or am I in it for the long game?

Turnkey investing is a patient investor's game. If you need a big, immediate return on your investment, then you need to focus on a different form of real estate investing such as wholesaling properties, lending money to active investors, or fixing and flipping houses. If you're more interested in building your long-term financial future, turnkey is right for you.

With turnkey, you can expect 5 to 7 percent for a cash-on-cash return, and 9 to 14 percent return if you use your leverage. These types of returns are excellent when you consider that done right, everything is done for you. However, this is not "get-rich-quick" kind of money. It is slow and steady, designed to build over time and provide steady income or wealth building. I'll dive into your purchasing and financing options as an investor a little later, which can certainly accelerate your ability to use turnkey real estate as a smart, long-term wealth strategy.

Do I need to be close to my investment, or can I handle the distance?

Will you be able to relax knowing that you have an investment property that you have trusted someone else to handle every detail of for you from a hundred or even thousands of miles away? This may be one of the more difficult questions to answer, because only you know how you are really going to feel. If you already know that you would like to drive past any investment property that you buy on a weekly basis, then turnkey real estate may be a waste of your money. You will be paying someone else to do the very job that you already know you will do weekly!

The question is only difficult because we have to be honest with ourselves. When we are honest, then the answer is simple. If you can't trust someone else to manage your investment, turnkey will drive you crazy. If you're comfortable leaving the keys in the hands of people you trust, you'll be fine.

Do I have enough money to get started?

It takes money to make money. You can't jump into turnkey investing with nothing. Anyone who says you can is selling snake oil. Buying passive investment properties is not a game you want to try to play with no money down or even with creative financing. Building a portfolio that truly changes the kind of future you can plan for yourself is going to take money. There is simply no way around that fact.

As an investor, you are looking for ways to reduce risk. I am going to share quite a bit about how to reduce risk when buying turnkey real estate. I am not going to waste our time together by telling you all the creative ways to get around not having money. Access to money and the important role it plays in building a strong turnkey portfolio is one risk that does not have a creative solution.

There are other ways to invest in real estate. There are other ways to build your cash reserves to use to buy real estate. So, while I will not waste our time together, I will advise you to be patient if you do not have the money yet to get started. Be patient. If you follow the steps I outline in this book, you can get started as a turnkey real estate investor and build your passive portfolio in any city, any market, and in any economic environment. The plan I share and the path I tell you to follow will work every time. So be patient and do whatever you need to do to build your cash reserves to get started with your turnkey portfolio.

If your honest answers to these questions reflect a long-term hands-off policy on your part, then turnkey real estate investing is a great option for you. And you're in the right place to learn how to do it well.

THE PATH TO TURNKEY INVESTING

The key to safely and passively investing in real estate is to follow the right steps. As long as you stay within tried-and-true guidelines, you will almost always come out on top in the end.

At Memphis Invest, we've created our own investing guidelines tailored to turnkey real estate. We call these guidelines the Turnkey Safely System™. Our process has seven steps:

1. Set your vision.

The first step in the system is to set your vision. You can't achieve your dreams if you don't have a clear idea of what those dreams are. When you identify exactly what you want to achieve, you can design your turnkey investments to help you reach those goals.

2. Research the market.

Turnkey gives you the ability to invest anywhere in the world. However, not all markets are created equal. Choosing a good market is critical to your long-term success as a real estate investor. Before you do anything else, you need to do your due diligence on potential locations.

3. Choose your turnkey company.

After you narrow down your markets, the fundamental key to success as an investor is selecting a high-quality turnkey company. This is a make-or-break aspect of turnkey real estate. You need a partner that is established, trustworthy, and reliable to manage your investments for you.

4. Create a plan for your investments.

Once you have a good turnkey company in your corner, that company will help you create a plan for your investments. Your plan is designed to turn your vision into a reality. Without a plan, you could come up short or find yourself in way over your head.

5. Make your investments.

Making your actual investments is the execution of your plan, and you need to be steady and systematic about it. Your turnkey company will help you with this stage of the process by presenting you with good potential investments and guiding you through the purchases.

6. Follow up with your investments.

Investing in passive real estate does not mean you're a passive investor. Mistakes do happen, and you need to stay up-to-date with the reports your turnkey partner sends you monthly. This is the stage of the process where you hold your turnkey company responsible for all the things it has promised you.

7. Expand your vision.

Turnkey real estate can expand with your vision for your future. You don't have to stop with one vision. You can always reach for the next horizon, and turnkey will be there to support your new goals.

Each chapter in this book covers one step in the Turnkey Safely System, and each step is a tool that can empower you to join the turnkey revolution and take your future into your own hands.

Every piece of this puzzle is indispensable. If you skip steps, you lose money.

This book also includes chapters on evaluating your purchasing options and using a self-directed IRA. By knowing all the different ways you can purchase a turnkey property, you can build your portfolio faster and always be prepared to take the next steps. The SDIRA is a special tool that can be a powerful part of your overall plan as an investor. If you spend time with this book and learn how to be a better, smarter passive real estate investor by following the process, you will set yourself up to win in real estate.

But as powerful as it is, you need more than the Turnkey Safely System alone to be a successful turnkey investor.

IT TAKES COURAGE

When you move to get started in turnkey, everyone around you is going to tell you what a fool you are. They won't just insist that buying real estate sight unseen is a bad decision—they'll say it's the worst decision you can make. Those naysayers are around us all the time. They said the same thing to me when I started investing in turnkey.

I spent many hours wringing my hands over what to do and should I get started or not. I spent a lot of wasted hours researching the wrong things and focusing my attention in the wrong areas. I even lost money to a mentor who was more interested in making money off my indecision rather than helping me get started in the right direction. Ultimately, it took me finding my own inner voice and the courage I needed to get started. I had to quit reading books until I "was ready" to get started. I had to quit listening to other investors who tried to convince me that I had to be actively involved in my properties or I would lose money. I had to make my own plan, set my own goals, and create my own vision and then take action! If I had continued to wait and listened to the naysayers, I would not be where I am today.

Don't just read about investing in real estate. Have the courage to act. Stand up and say, "I took the steps to learn how to do this. I am going to implement a strategy, and I'm going to change the trajectory of my future."

Now is the time to make it happen. But where do you start? I'm about to show you.

If you don't believe that there's a reason behind what you're doing and why you're doing it, you won't find the courage you need to move forward. In the next chapter, I'll show you how to define a clear vision that motivates you to take the necessary steps to achieve your dreams.

THE TURNKEY SAFELY CHECKLIST

Is Turnkey Right for Me?

🔑 Do I want to be hands-on or hands-off with my investments?

🔑 Do I want a quick return, or am I in it for the long game?

🔑 Do I need to be close to my investment, or can I handle the distance?

🔑 Do I have enough money to get started?

TURNKEY MASTERY TIPS

Creative financing is *not* a good option when you buy turnkey real estate.

If you are not ready financially to invest passively, spend time building your cash. This is not a short-term, quick investment, so do not use creative financing such as money partners, hard money lenders, or borrowing from credit cards. These strategies can work for short-term investments, but not for long-term passive investments such as turnkey.

Follow the steps!

If you are stuck after setting your vision and worried that it may be too big or even not big enough and don't know where to start, follow the steps! Taking the simple action of picking a market to research can be enough to push past your fear and get the ball rolling!

SET YOUR VISION

My brother, Kent Clothier, tells one of the most powerful stories of vision I've ever heard. Let me give you a little background on Kent before telling you the story.

As my older brother, Kent has always been an inspiration, mentor, and, occasionally, a thorn in my side. Like most brothers, we grew up supporting, then fighting, then supporting each other again. No one could mess with his little brother but him. He was always one of the most focused and driven people I have ever been around. Those times when he was a thorn in my side usually revolved around his pushing me to be better, try harder, and become more focused.

Kent has always had the Midas touch, and he joined our dad straight out of high school in the family business. He excelled quickly and was soon helping to build a $50 million annual sales grocery company in the heart of Memphis. He was a natural leader.

Our dad sold that company to a larger firm in the mid-nineties, and Kent had the opportunity of a lifetime. He found himself in South Florida taking over as the vice president of sales at one of the largest privately held companies in the state. This was no ordinary company either. It was doing $800 million annually. The number of people Kent was leading went from 40 to over 200. Kent not only accepted the challenge: as usual, he crushed it. He took that company with $800 million in annual sales and turned it into a $2 billion company in three years.

Then, due to a series of bad decisions and, as Kent will tell you, his own inexperience and youth, Kent and the company parted ways. My brother wasn't worried. Kent had more than doubled sales at that business, and he thought he was the guy everybody wanted. As he likes to put it, "I thought $800,000 jobs grew on trees."

He was wrong.

The next two years were the hardest of Kent's life. Kent relocated to Memphis for a period and worked with a business partner to grow their company into a competitor of his former company. That idea was short-lived, as bad luck seemed to be following him at this point. The man with the Midas touch suddenly found himself unable to right his ship. The man who at one point had over $1 million in the bank now found himself living on the edge of financial ruin.

At his lowest point, Kent packed everything he owned into his Ford Explorer and drove back down to Ft. Lauderdale, Florida. He managed to bounce back and start a new real estate company from the ground up. He poured himself into building a new business unlike any that he had built in the past. He attended seminars, invested his time and money into marketing, and showed again that he was willing to outwork anyone, but even then, he was just surviving. He had a new house and a new wife, yet no legacy, no retirement, and nothing for his young daughter's college fund. He knew he had to make a change.

LEARNING TO GET VULNERABLE

We hear it all the time today, "You have to get vulnerable if you want to succeed." But what does that really mean? In Kent's case, it meant he had to own up to and then forgive his mistakes. He had to chart a new course forward that didn't include beating himself up for mistakes. He had to forgive himself for thinking that he was invincible and especially for believing that his gift wasn't something to be protected. It meant he had to open up and get strong advice from people who had been down the path he wanted to go; from the top to the bottom and back to the top again.

Finally, during one of their talks, a mentor of his gave him an exercise. "You need a vision," he told Kent. "Try this. Sit down and write out your perfect day. Every detail of it. Don't leave anything out. Don't sell yourself short and write a few paragraphs. Really dig in and open up about the sights, the sounds, the smells . . . all of the details you can imagine in your perfect day."

Kent took the next few days and followed the advice. He wrote in vivid detail about a day where he woke up without an alarm clock. A day where he and his wife enjoyed breakfast and coffee together before waking their daughter up for school. In Kent's perfect day, he and his wife got into a nice vehicle with their daughter in the backseat and dropped her off at school together. Then they drove to a hotel nearby to pick up clients they loved—people who had come into town to work with them on a mentorship—and took them down the A1A along the Florida coast to Kent's brand-new offices. There, they would introduce the clients to their team and spend the whole day networking and building a business plan.

Kent wrote that perfect day about a company that didn't exist, a vehicle that didn't exist, and clients that didn't exist. His wife worked for someone else at the time, and they never took their daughter to school together. But he wrote down every word that he could see in his mind's eye just as his mentor had told him. He spent every day reading his vision without fail, for nine months. He recorded himself reading it and committed every detail to memory. In his mind, he was living his perfect day every day.

Then, one morning, he and his wife were driving down the A1A in South Florida with a couple from Amarillo, Texas, in the backseat of their nice Lincoln Navigator. They were coaching students who were paying Kent to mentor them as real estate investors and had flown into town the night before. Kent and his wife picked them up after dropping their daughter off at school, and they were on their way to Kent's brand-new office building in Boca Raton that he'd leased four weeks prior.

That was when it hit him. He almost drove off the road.

"What are you doing!" his wife gasped as Kent righted the car. "Do we have a flat tire?"

"No," Kent told her, "this is my perfect day. I wrote about this nine months ago. I have read this to myself every day. I have listened to it while working out. I dedicated myself to living my perfect day, and I was so close to it that I didn't realize it was actually happening!"

Kent had taken the time to visualize every detail of how he wanted his life to be. He spent his time working to make it happen. Every day, he told himself that he could do it. Every day, he told himself that his vision was not only possible, it was already real. Realizing the power of vision, Kent didn't rest on his laurels. He kept reinventing his perfect day again and again, making changes and improvements each time. As his life grew, his vision grew. Today, Kent has two daughters and a son and lives on the cliffs overlooking the ocean. His vision is well beyond simply driving his kids to school and having an office. He designed the ultimate lifestyle through the power of vision.

THE POWER OF VISION

When you create a very specific image of where you're going, everything else falls into place.

Vision is at the heart of the turnkey revolution. Your vision is your "why" for doing what you do as an investor. You can usually spot your "why" by looking at the things that keep you up at night. "Why am I doing this every day? What is it I'm looking for? Why am I exploring the option of building wealth by investing in real estate?" The answer to those questions is your vision.

For example, maybe you want to provide for your family and put your children through college. Maybe you want to leave a legacy for your grandkids. Maybe you want to buy yourself a retirement that gives you the ability to wake up when you want to wake up, travel where you want to travel, and experience the things you want to experience. Remember, my first house was not just bricks and sticks with an address for me. It represented my sons' college fund. It represented a very important "why" for me.

Whatever the case, your vision is your inspiration for getting up and doing what you do every day. It keeps you moving forward. Without a clear vision to motivate you, you may never take action in the first place. Or worse, you may go on a crazy binge of investments without knowing what you're doing and lose everything.

Everybody has a vision inside of him or her. You just have to dig it up, get clear about it, and act on it. Some may be thinking to themselves right about now, "*That* is the first step in buying turnkey real estate? Create a vision? I thought this was about real estate investing!"

This is all about real estate investing. I have worked with thousands of investors at this point, and more than a small share of those investors have no real vision as to why they are investing in the first place. "To get rich" is not a vision. "Because my friend owns a lot of property" is not a vision. "My boss said real estate is a great investment" is not a vision. And yet, those are just a few of the reasons I have been told time and again from interested real estate investors.

Setting a strong vision is the first step in the Turnkey Safely System. In this chapter, I'll teach you the difference between vision and goals and show you how to set both of them in a powerful way that will propel you to success.

VISION VERSUS GOALS

A vision is the ultimate picture of what you want to achieve. A vision can be as much about how you feel as it is about where you are or what you have. However, just because you imagine that picture doesn't mean it's going to come to life on its own.

That's where goals come into play.

Your goals are the stepping-stones to your vision. They're the concrete plan that's going to take you from point A to point B. While a vision is fairly static, your goals are always changing as you get closer and closer to where you want to be. This is a major mistake that many people make, not just real estate investors. They fail to adapt and change along the way. You have a road map, and at times there will be detours. You still have the same vision. You still have the same ending point that you are trying to get to. Smart investors take stock along the way and adjust their goals to make sure they are always on the correct course.

Your vision and your goals work together to help you reach success. Defining a strong vision gives you the clarity you need to guide your decisions and set goals that will take you where you want to go. Goals, meanwhile, work as milestones of measurement that keep you accountable to your vision. That is the reason for constantly evaluating and adjusting.

On the hard days when you feel like you're making no headway, your goals can be a powerful reality check. You can look at your track record of hitting those milestones and say, "All right, what have I accomplished so far? Have I hit a few of these milestones yet?" Most of the time, the answer is yes—and your motivation to keep moving forward is renewed. This is a really important point to remember as a turnkey real estate investor because your positive milestones may be far apart. They may not all be measured by the size of a bank account.

So, it is important to be aware of where you are and celebrate every time you win.

CELEBRATE ALL WINS

What does it mean to celebrate all wins, and why is it so important for turnkey investors? Celebrating all wins means giving yourself a little pat on the back—or a big pat on the back for a big win—every time something good happens. Believe me, in real estate, there are plenty of opportunities to wish something had gone differently. A smart investor is the one who understands that this is a long game. A marathon if you will, not a sprint.

These are small celebrations I am talking about, not buying expensive big-face watches or the car of your dreams. There may be time for that at some point in the future, but along the way to creating your vision, it's also important to keep perspective and not lose focus on the big picture.

Celebrating all wins means treating yourself to a nice dinner at your favorite restaurant when you buy your first property. If your goals include having a portfolio of five properties in certain amount of time, and you hit it, then celebrate by buying that bottle of wine that is a little more expensive or getting out of town for the weekend.

Along the way to realizing your vision, you need to celebrate *all* wins, including even the small ones. The month when every rent payment is in on time is a good reason to go spend some time with your favorite people. The small wins will one day add up to a really big vision, and you want to make sure to celebrate as you make your way.

HOW TO SET YOUR VISION AND GOALS

With real estate investing, as with most things in life, you need both a strong vision and a strong set of goals to achieve success. So how do you set an effective vision and effective goals?

Set your vision.

Two key things define a strong vision. First, it reflects your "why." It reflects the strongest part of your reason for wanting to achieve in the first place. Second, it focuses on you.

If you don't know your "why," ask yourself this question: What two or three things would you keep if you had to give up everything else? Is it your family—your spouse and your children? Is it your volunteer work at the soup kitchen or local orphanage? Is it your dune buggy, because you live in the desert and your passion in life is racing that vehicle over the sand?

Whatever you choose to hold onto is what you really desire in life. It's also your reason for investing, because no matter what you want to do or have, you need money for it. It takes money to provide for your family. It takes money to support yourself while you volunteer. It takes money to have a bigger impact in your volunteer work. It takes money to participate in your hobbies. The bigger the hobby, the more money it takes to support your passion. Your decisions as an investor need to support those ideals.

The second key to vision is that it must be about you. If your vision is to volunteer at an orphanage, that's great—but you have to want it because you get a personal sense of fulfillment from doing that. Never use your vision to convince yourself and the world that you deserve the money and the life you want. It truly has to be your passion. And it's okay to be completely materialistic about this. If you like nice cars and your dream is to own a completely restored '69 red Mustang convertible, then that car should be in your vision.

Your vision cannot be vague. It needs to be complete and detailed. To create your vision, you can use the same exercise that Kent's mentor taught him: What is your perfect day?

When you create your perfect day, be as specific as you can, and don't leave anything out. Close your eyes. Ask yourself: What do I hear and feel when I wake up in the morning? How long do I lie in bed after I wake up? What do I cook for breakfast, and whom do I cook it for? What does it smell like? What music is on in the background? Describe every part of the experience in detail from start to finish.

Kent challenged me some years ago to go through this exercise myself. He challenged me to spend some time thinking about what my perfect day would look like. He challenged me to be specific and detailed and not to worry if it sounded hokey. It also has to be real. Meaning that, unfortunately, you cannot go back in time. You cannot share a meal with someone from your past who is no longer with you. Those types of experiences, while they may be something that you desperately want, are not going to happen. So, focus on what *can* happen. Focus on the feelings, the experiences, the sights, sounds, and smells that you can experience. By way of example, here is an excerpt from my personal perfect day:

There it is . . . the familiar sound of the morning tides coming in and crashing on the beach below. I open my eyes as my body begins to awaken. I take a moment to really explore my body with my mind and assess how I am feeling, what I am hearing, what I am smelling. The drapes flow into the room from the strong ocean breeze and let the dim light from the rising sun peek in. I can hear the ocean birds singing among the sounds of the waves. I notice the faint smell of the fresh flowers we have planted on the patio in full bloom, even though their fragrance is mostly overpowered by the salt air. The air is cool, and I smile as I realize my wife has taken the blanket from the bed and rolled it around her, leaving my skin to cool in the morning air. No alarm clocks to wake us, just the sounds and smells of nature and the little feet of our children that climbed into our bed sometime during the night. I pull myself up from the bed and take in the room as I hear the coffee maker with its familiar grind go off downstairs. I am sore from my recent race and feeling a bit stiff, but happy to be competing at my age. I feel strong. I sit on the side of the bed and go through my morning routine of finding three things I am grateful for. I know I will write these in my daily calendar shortly, but right now I concentrate on being thankful that I woke up this morning, thankful that I am in good physical condition and can still run, and thankful for my wonderful, healthy family.

Take this exercise seriously. My perfect day is 12 pages long. I spent an entire day working on it that I set aside just for that purpose, and I've been reading it once or twice a month ever since. I have tweaked it several times as I get older and little parts of my perfect day come to fruition. I follow the same advice I gave you earlier and always adjust my goals to fit my vision. The main part of my vision never changes, but as I have gotten older and welcomed five beautiful kids into my world, it has changed a bit. No matter how I have changed it, though, I intend to live that perfect day 365 days a year, and every day I get closer to it.

When you set a clear vision and keep reminding yourself where you want to go, you put yourself on track for success as a real estate investor. Investing in passive real estate as a turnkey investor is your vehicle to building real wealth and allowing yourself to experience your perfect day.

Set your goals.

If your vision answers the question why, then your goals answer the question how. They are your plan for getting from where you are to where you want to go.

You know your vision. Now you just need to ask yourself, "How do I accomplish it?" The difference between the investors who achieve their visions and those who don't is that the latter group stops right here. You may write a very eloquent perfect day, but unless you follow that up by asking, "How do I get there?" you will never have the means to live the authentic life you want to live.

How do you set strong goals? A great way to do it is to work backward. Take that vision of where you want to go and calculate exactly how much income you need to live your perfect life. That answer will be different for everyone because money may not be the biggest factor in achieving your personal vision. However, it is important that you work backward to measure your goals against your vision.

I'm not talking about vague ideas here. The same way that your vision needs to be detailed, your goals need to be specific and realistic. One of the biggest problems people have with goal setting is that they tend to work with fantasy numbers. Instead of sitting down and figuring out exactly what they need to achieve their vision, they pull a fantasy number out of the air and say, "I want to make a million bucks a year. That sounds good."

While a million bucks a year does sound good, it also sounds like a fairy tale. Don't fall into that trap. Fantasy numbers will never take you to your final destination, because they're not consistent or realistic. Instead, take the time to run the numbers and compare them to your vision. If your vision is to retire, then look at the amount of money you take home after taxes today, and ask yourself, "Do I need more than this when I retire?" Probably not, and you're probably going to have fewer liabilities when you retire than you do now, because certain things you own will be paid off.

Maybe your vision is to provide a dream wedding for your daughter or pay for your kids' college tuition. Maybe you want to give each of your kids a home free and clear as a present to help them with their start as adults in the future. Quality of life in retirement and the ability to have a huge impact on your children and their education are incredible visions to have. The great thing is, you do not have to choose between one and the other. A high-quality passive investment portfolio bought through the turnkey process can help make your vision a reality. All you have to do is the math to figure out how much you will need to reach it.

Take that number and scale it up. Figure out how much you really need to retire. Most of the time, you'll look at that number and say, "That's all?" Studies show that most people need only $10,000 a month to have the kind of retirement they want. You look at that and you realize, "Wow, I only need to own six properties free and clear to make that happen. I don't need 20 houses after all."

From there, each of those six properties becomes one of your goals. You know that you need to buy one house every X number of months to own all six free and clear by the time you retire. You know that you need X number of dollars to buy the house. You know what you need to do to earn that money—and you act on it.

Just like that, you're on the path to transforming your vision into your reality.

THE FORESIGHT TO SUCCEED

I met a great woman named Karen who flagged me down after a turnkey presentation I made several years ago in South Florida. "I loved your talk," she said, excited. "I want to liquidate all my other investments and put the money into turnkey properties with you guys. Let's look at some properties. I'm ready to sign the contracts today."

"All right, slow down," I said. "Let's talk about this."

I needed to slow her down before we could go any further. An excited real estate investor, making decisions based on emotion and excitement, is going to have a hard time asking good questions. An excited investor is not going to make a quality decision. I needed to get her focused and learn as much as I could about her needs and get her onto the right path. I started with a couple of simple questions.

TURNKEY MASTERY TIPS

Look for a partner that takes the time to listen and learn.

If you want to build a portfolio of turnkey properties and do it safely, you want to do business with a trustworthy company, right? Right off the bat, pay attention to how urgent the company's people are to get you into buying mode. Pay attention to how quickly they are trying

to get you warmed up and writing checks for properties. You definitely want to find a company that is going
to be your partner. The best thing your partner can do
is go slow and spend some time getting to know you
as an investor. There is no way a turnkey company can
build a portfolio that fits your needs perfectly if they are
not taking time to listen and learn!

"What are you trying to achieve with your investments?
What's your vision?"

It turned out that Karen had some ideas. She was ready to
retire. In fact, she had already retired and was burning through
the retirement funds she had worked so hard to save. She also
wanted to leave a legacy for her daughter and granddaughter—
but she didn't have a clear vision, and she didn't know exactly
what it would take to achieve her goals.

Together, we figured out what her vision really was. We got
really clear, really quickly. Karen did not want to go back to
work, and it was very important to her to spend time with her
daughter and granddaughter. When all was said and done, she
wanted to leave a legacy.

Next, we looked through her investments. She had spent a
lot of time going to investment clubs and had quite an assort-
ment of investments going. Some were making her money,
and others were losing her money. She had spent quite a bit
of money already on advisors and had very little to show for it
other than DIY programs sitting on her shelves.

I advised her to keep the investments that were performing well, and she decided to drop the underperformers in
favor of buying turnkey properties with our company. We also
looked at how many properties she would need and found that
she would have additional investment dollars left over. With
that money, Karen was able to make short-term loans to earn

interest on her money but also to stay flexible if need be. It was a mix of investments that provided protection for her remaining money, allowed for her to have several different cash flow streams each month, and left her with time to visit her family. She went home and executed her plan immediately. A few short months later, she had a solid plan working for her vision and a new outlook on her future.

From that day on, Karen no longer flew blind with her investments. Instead, she had a concrete path to the life she really wanted.

If you don't know where you want to go, you'll never know when you get there. A clear vision and a strong set of goals will take you a long way as an investor. Take the time to create them right, and then move forward. You should always be taking steady, patient action in the direction of your vision. As long as you keep the big picture in view and remain methodical about your decisions, one day you're going to look up like Kent did and realize, "Wow—I'm here."

But as important as they are, your vision and goals are only the beginning of the turnkey revolution. Once you have them in place, it's time to get to the nuts and bolts of investing in turnkey real estate. The first thing we have to do is get our finances and our understanding of the best ways to purchase our properties in order.

I am going to take the next couple of chapters and break down the boring stuff! However, it is super important if we want to build a really good portfolio. After all, what is the point of creating a vision and setting goals if we don't understand exactly what it takes to get there? We have to understand all of the different ways we can start building our portfolio and the power of strategies using leverage, tax advantages, and even our retirement savings accounts.

So, stay with me. Let's knock out the basics of financing, taxes, and retirement accounts in the next two chapters, and then we are on to the fun stuff.

THE TURNKEY SAFELY CHECKLIST

Finding Your "Why"

🔑 What is most important to me? What two or three things would I keep if I had to give up everything else?

🔑 What does my perfect day look like?

Setting a Path

🔑 What are the top five investing goals that will take me to my vision?

1. _____

   _____

2. _____

   _____

3. _____

   _____

4. _____

   _____

5. _____

   _____

TURNKEY MASTERY TIPS

Take steady, patient action in the direction of your vision.

Never confuse simply making changes with making progress. In the case of Karen, she was ready to change everything because she thought that was what she needed to do to move forward and make progress toward her goals. But what she really needed was some clarity to help fine-tune her investments. Change is not necessarily a sign of making progress.

CHAPTER 3

DEMYSTIFYING MONEY— HOW TO FINANCE YOUR TURNKEY PORTFOLIO

I'm sure if you're reading this book, you would already agree that investing in real estate can be a profitable and exciting venture. For most people, it's a sound way to build toward their vision. As we explored in the last chapter, that vision can be all about retirement. For others, real estate is a way to create an extra stream of income that ultimately allows them to pursue their passions. That is their version of vision. No matter what your vision and goals are, if real estate investing is part of your plan, you have to understand how to use financing to help you succeed.

Whatever your reason for wanting to invest in real estate, it's ultimately about creating income and freedom and achieving peace of mind while doing it. I will spend a lot of time talking about risks that come with real estate. Some of those risks are magnified by the turnkey investment process, and others are mitigated. In the end, the ability to finance a property right off the bat can both reduce and increase risk. So, it has to be done carefully and correctly.

How do you know it's going to be a worthy venture? There are a lot of real estate gurus out there making big promises about how easy it is to invest in real estate. They'll promise to make you millions with zero effort. And honestly, that's just a scam!

Investing in real estate is simple. It is only made simpler by investing with a good turnkey real estate company. But that does not mean easy or hands-off. As I've already shown you, digging into the details and being patient are both an important part of the process, and we have to do it with financing as well.

I am going to help you know the ins and outs of making smart decisions when buying your turnkey properties: how much you need to start, how you can make the most of what you have, what pitfalls to watch for, and everything you need to start your financial future off on the right foot.

TOP FINANCIAL QUESTIONS WHEN GETTING STARTED

First, here are some important questions for when you are getting started.

Question 1: How much money do I need to start?

Starting off, there's not really a set baseline for every investor to follow. After all, there are a lot of factors that go into how much money you need to get started: where you're investing, for example. Markets vary widely! The amount of money you need to invest in New York City is wildly different from what you need to invest in Kansas City.

TURNKEY MASTERY TIPS

Cheap properties are not good turnkey investments.

Take a moment and underline the next sentence. Do not buy "cheap" properties! Now, if you're taking notes in a separate notebook, write that sentence down. If not, grab a pen and write it in the margins. This is extremely important if you want to build a passive turnkey portfolio of properties. Cheap means less expensive, smaller properties in more impoverished areas of the city. These are not good turnkey investment properties. These properties are a favorite of scam companies that prey on out-of-area investors. They are inexpensive, easy to get, and there are plenty available. These properties are better left to local, active investors able to put their time into the management and operation of these low-cost, cheap houses. A quality turnkey property will never be priced less than $60,000. Don't be fooled by promises of low prices and high returns. If it sounds easy to make a double-digit return, then don't even consider it for your turnkey portfolio. It is never easy, and quality turnkey investments are not "cheap properties."

Here's what you need to keep in mind when planning for how much money you need to get started:

- What kind of properties do I want to invest in?
- What markets do I want to invest in?
- What kind of safety net do I want to have?

- Am I anticipating every cost?

- What risks are there?

- What insurance do I need?

- What is my financing strategy?

Let's break it down further. One of the first things to consider is your financing strategy. How are you planning to pay for your properties? Are you going to go with traditional bank financing and a 25 percent down payment, or are you looking to pay all at once with an all-cash offer?

If you're buying a $100,000 property, that's the difference between needing the full $100,000 or just $25,000 to acquire the home. Now, right off the bat you may be wondering why I use 25 percent down instead of 20 percent. Well, if you are going to use traditional financing to build a portfolio, 25 percent is the amount I suggest you put down on a property. When you put 25 percent down, you are not penalized with fees by your lender or FNMA for putting too little down. You read that right. If you want to put less than 25 percent down on a traditional mortgage, you can. But there is going to be a penalty for the right to do that.

On top of any fees you will pay, there will also be mortgage insurance you have to pay monthly until your balance is equal to 75 percent of the value of your property. You get penalized twice—first with fees and then with a monthly charge.

There are other practical reasons to put more down when you purchase a property as well. It can help you to negotiate better interest rates and lower closing costs. It also increases your equity position in the property from day one and decreases your monthly payment since you are borrowing less money.

Lastly, after purchasing four properties for your portfolio, for each additional property you purchase with a FNMA backed loan, you will be required to put 25 percent down without exceptions. You might as well get started on the right foot from the beginning and anticipate putting 25 percent down.

But buying the property is just part of the puzzle. As an investor, there are other costs you need to consider. Besides the initial down payment, you have to consider:

- The interest rate
- Home inspection
- Home appraisal
- Closing costs
- Property taxes
- Insurance costs
- Maintenance and property management

These are all hard costs. You should expect to have these costs with every property you purchase. Some come at the beginning when you are buying and others occur throughout the life of your property, but they all have one thing in common: they will definitely occur. They will vary based on where you are buying, and as I will constantly remind you through the book, you must do your due diligence. You have to know these basic costs on each property you put in your portfolio.

The No Big Deal Fund

A big question investors have when researching turnkey real estate is how much to keep in a rainy-day fund. That is a big question with a different answer for each investor. How you answer it will depend on your vision. I also think it is the wrong question to ask yourself.

If you have to keep a rainy-day fund, then you may be buying real estate for the wrong reasons. The fundamental reason to buy real estate is to earn a positive income on the property. The second reason is to protect your capital.

Rather than asking how much to keep in a rainy-day fund, ask instead if you have enough money to purchase a property, earn a positive income yearly from the property, and feel comfortable that you can cover any expenses should they come up. Expenses to think about may include covering your monthly mortgage when a property is vacant (it will happen) and covering any maintenance costs that will invariably come up. You never know when expenses will come or when a monthly income will disappear for a time. These are not *if* scenarios, but *when* scenarios.

Don't view the money for these expenses as rainy-day funds. Prepare for them in advance and look at them as the "no big deal fund." Such expenses are just a normal occurrence in business and are why you followed this book to select the best turnkey company you can find: to handle these issues for you.

Make sure from the very beginning of creating your vision that you are honest with yourself about exactly where you stand financially. If you need monthly cash flow from a real estate property to cover your bills, you are not ready to invest in real estate. Do not put yourself in a position to need the monthly income. Be patient and work hard to be in a great position to invest in turnkey real estate.

If you don't have the funds to take care of problems, you're going to be dead in the water. If you have a means to handle problems, you're not only going to be less stressed, but you're going to be better equipped to succeed.

Here is an example of closing costs on a typical $100,000 rental property:

Down payment: $25,000 (25 percent of purchase price)

Closing costs: $4,500

Total investment: $29,500

With that in mind, you can start to consider how much you may need to start investing in real estate. Remember, though, depending on your vision, one property is not going to do it. If you do not have the funds in place to purchase more than one property, you need to have a plan for how you are going to generate funds consistently to build your portfolio.

What about repair costs? If you are buying a property from a turnkey company and it is not covering all renovation cost, then it is not a turnkey company. You should be purchasing properties that are already renovated and are either generating income or being marketed for a resident. You should never buy properties where you are expected to pay for the renovation. That is not a turnkey property. That is a nightmare!

Question 2: Where does the income come from in real estate?

When investing in rental properties, you need to make sure that your properties will provide a stable and reliable return. That is the purpose of turnkey real estate: providing a stable and reliable return passively. So how does a turnkey real estate investor actually earn the return? Where does the money come from?

1. **Rental payments.** Your residents pay rent every month. This is your bread and butter investment income. You can maximize your rental income by investing in higher quality properties, upgrading your property values through continuous upkeep, and adding new single-family properties to your portfolio. Remember: vacancies eliminate your rental income until you find a new resident. This is the most expensive time period for any investor, so quality property management and a highly focused team are essential to your turnkey investing success!

2. **Property appreciation.** Even for your average homeowner, real estate is said to be one of the best investments you can make. That's because real estate appreciates. You can buy a property, improve it, wait for it to appreciate, and sell for a profit years down the line. While you're not flipping, you can wait for ideal conditions down the line and make a profit. Appreciation can be risky, but if you're paying attention to your market's economic trends and are ahead of the curve, you could be buying in an area ripe for revitalization—and that can really pay off!

This is where your income comes from with turnkey real estate—the rental payments and appreciation of your property. One thing to pay close attention to when you first get started is how your turnkey partner renovates and upkeeps properties. Does it believe in maximizing value by keeping properties clean and up to date? This will be important for you as an investor.

A property that is well maintained and taken care of will increase in value much quicker than a property managed by a company that focuses on cutting corners and holding down costs. The benefits of keeping your property in top-notch shape come sharply into focus when you look at your two income streams. The best properties attract the highest rent and appreciate the fastest. Period.

Question 3: How to finance your investments?

There are a few different avenues you can take to finance your turnkey investments. The options really come down to your personal situation and preferences. There are pros and cons to each, and sometimes you may have to go with one over the other.

Most Common: Bank Loan with a Down Payment

This is what most people think of when they imagine buying real estate. Getting approved by the bank, making a 25 percent down payment, so on. The positive here is that you aren't having to pay for the whole cost of the property up front. That does give you a degree of leverage, because you are using the bank's money, not your own.

However, you are going to be dealing with a mortgage, and the cost is going to eat into your monthly profits. One thing to really pay attention to is your interest rate. Interest will be the single largest expense you have over the life of your loan. A big advantage of using a bank loan is the ability to turn one dollar into three dollars.

Turning One Dollar into Three Dollars

This is a powerful strategy that every real estate investor should utilize to some degree. You can turn $1 into $3 if you can leverage your turnkey property purchase. Instead of needing $100,000 to purchase one property, an investor can divide that $100,000 into three different properties with financing. That includes enough money to put 25 percent down and pay all closing costs while even leaving a few dollars for the no big deal fund.

In the end, you own three properties instead of one. You have turned $100,000 dollars into $300,000 worth of investment property. This is how a turnkey investor can quickly build a powerful portfolio. So, how do you go about getting a loan from a bank so you can leverage your money?

When you're getting a loan, there are four primary factors that a bank will look at to determine whether or not you qualify:

- **Credit score.** You saw this one coming. You should have a score over 600, or be prepared to be hit with extra fees. Investors, be prepared to be required to score higher. You'll be under more scrutiny.

- **Tax returns.** If you didn't claim much income on your last tax return, it will negatively impact your chances of approval.

- **Employment.** It's not just about having a job, it's about your reliability at said job. Banks typically are looking for you to be at your place of employment for a minimum of two years. If you have changed jobs but remained in the same or similar field, it likely won't raise any red flags.

- **Debt-to-income ratio.** Whether it's credit card debt or another mortgage, your track record with debt is very telling to your future lenders. There's not a set standard for what is okay and what is not—it depends on the loan! Still, all the more reason to have your debts in order.

Also remember that you need to find a lender that won't hinder your borrowing. And by that, we mean a lender that follows Fannie Mae guidelines will make it a lot more difficult for you to borrow after you've financed four properties (the traditional limit).

In 2009, Fannie Mae rolled out the 5–10 Properties Financed Program to help stimulate the economy through investors.

This increased the limit to 10 properties, but only in banks that adopted the program. Make sure you know where your bank stands, or you could run into difficulty down the line!

Best Offer: All Cash, Up Front

You could avoid the hassle of mortgages, credit scores, and interest rates altogether—just pay the whole amount up front. What are the advantages to this? For one, it makes for an incredibly attractive offer. Many times, you can use the fact that you are paying cash for a property as a negotiating tool.

You also have the advantage of it being a "one and done" situation. Once you close on the property, you're not going to have to deal with a monthly mortgage payment. Apart from repairs and other various property expenses, your rental income is going to be pure income.

However, you do lose out on leverage. It's all your money on the table, and that can be a lot riskier.

One word of caution. If a company requires you to pay all cash, that may not be a good indication of its product or the strength of the company. The company could be having cash flow issues and need to close properties quickly. Waiting for a lender may not be something it wants to do. At the same time, its properties may not stand up to much scrutiny. Certainly not the scrutiny of an inspection and appraisal. The company may not be pulling permits on the work it is doing to the property. For any number of reasons, very few of them good, a company may require you to pay all cash. This is good cause to slow down, ask a few more questions, and dig a little deeper.

Best Leverage: Private or Hard Money Lending

In real estate, you can take advantage of leverage—so, why wouldn't you? Hard money lending utilizes the money of individuals with a professional interest in you—perhaps other investors or professionals who see potential in you. You may have to have a pretty strong pitch and track record to impress them!

Similar but different, there are private money lenders. These tend to be friends, family, or acquaintances that you can charm or build personal relationship with, who then lend you the money you need to purchase your investment properties.

You still have to pay them back, keep in mind—but there's room to negotiate on a timeline, interest rate, and other details, where you may be more locked in without much wiggle room with your bank.

Most turnkey companies are not going to care which method of purchase you use. This is your transaction, and as long as you can perform and close the contract you are going to be able to dictate whether you pay cash or use leverage. At the very beginning, when you are planning out your vision and goals, how you are going to buy the properties has to be at the front of your mind. Remember, this is not a get-rich-quick strategy. This is about preserving and growing what you have worked hard to get. Think carefully and plan for how you are going to buy your property.

Best Opportunity: Self-Directed Investment Retirement Accounts

Self-directed retirement accounts are one of the best resources a turnkey real estate investor can use to build a passive portfolio. In fact, self-directed IRA accounts are so specialized and specific in regard to using them to buy real estate, plus a favorite with turnkey real estate investors, that I am including an entire chapter on them!

Question 4: When should I start scaling my portfolio?

So, you've purchased a property, completed renovations, and you've been renting it out for a while. How do you know when it's time to start expanding your business? There are a few things to know about "having your house in order" before you jump into buying more than four or five properties. Some investors are too cavalier about scaling and wind up in over their heads. I feel strongly that four to five properties are a nice portfolio and a great start. This is a spot that many investors dream to be in.

Build a nice portfolio and then observe. Learn how it is going to perform over a few months or even a year before making more moves. Allow the turnkey partner you have chosen to work with earn your trust and the right to build a larger portfolio. Too often investors want to jump in with both feet very quickly. Don't make the same mistake!

Getting the Most out of the Properties You Have

One mistake investors make is not capitalizing on the investments they already have. If you aren't maximizing your profits and have a lot of untapped potential, you shouldn't continue to build your portfolio just yet.

First, get the most out of what you have. Get things firing on all cylinders. That means renovations, upgrades, and getting value. Premium value. Can you push your property values and what you can charge for rent based on those values? Ask potential turnkey partners how they protect you and maximize your value. You are listening for an answer that mixes pressing your rents to maximum levels without squeezing quality residents out of the property. In residential real estate, rarely are rental increases worth forcing a vacancy.

Planning for the Unexpected

Remember that no big deal fund we mentioned earlier? You definitely still need to be able to operate from a point of not worrying about the no big deal expense days. They are coming. You should be strong enough to accept that they are coming and use your rental property income wisely. Reduce debt on the properties. Perform all needed and required upkeep. So long as you can cover vacancies and basic maintenance, you don't need a rainy-day fund. You simply need to be smart about how you build wealth with your income so when expenses hit . . . they are no big deal!

As you plan to expand, it is important to remember that your finances are about to take a hit with the acquisition of a new property. Your ability to handle the costs of ownership should reflect that. If you are unsure, don't make a move yet. Wait until you are strong enough to build your portfolio.

Whatever happens, you want any and all mistakes to stay contained—they don't need to sink the whole ship. Be a smart, prepared investor on the front end, and there will be no need for a separate fund.

Question 5: What about the taxes?

There are few cases in which we like the sound of "tax." One of those cases is when it comes paired with "benefits." For real estate investors, the tax benefits are plentiful. If you know how to navigate them, you can find considerable tax savings—even tax shelters.

That said, wading through taxes without the help of a CPA can be overwhelming. There are many tax breaks you could potentially be taking advantage of, but there are also traps and mistakes to be on the lookout for! I am only going to make a few comments and suggestions here. Make sure that you consult a CPA or a tax professional before assuming any advantages with your investments.

Deductions

For both investors and property managers, there are deductions to take advantage of. For your rental properties, you can write off many of the costs associated with mortgage interest, property tax, depreciation, repairs, and operating expenses. For the investor, you can deduct the mortgage interest on your primary and sometimes secondary residence. Repairs can also be written off, as they do not add value to your property.

If you're an investor working from home, don't forget deductions you can take for your dedicated home office space and other work expenses, like phone and Internet. If you invest out of state, which is the beauty of turnkey real estate—you can literally invest anywhere in the world—track your travel expenses. You may be able to deduct those expense when you travel to see your properties. Just remember to itemize carefully and consult a professional accountant—particularly one who is experienced in dealing with real estate investors.

You want someone experienced in your particular situation, as she will help ensure you don't make mistakes or miss out on any tax benefits and savings.

Capital Gains

Sold any property lately? You need to know about capital gains and taxes! Short-term capital gains apply to properties sold that were held for less than a year. You will have to pay taxes on that income from the sold property based on your tax bracket.

For investors, you want to stick to long-term gains as much as possible. They apply to properties held for a year or more, are taxed at a lower rate, and there's even a capital gains exclusion that you may be able to take advantage of if you earned less than $500,000 in profits on your property.

Depreciation

Have you held your residential rental property for less than 27.5 years? You can take advantage of depreciation! You can recover some of the costs of your property yearly through tax deductions, even if your property is producing positive cash flow. The IRS does have guidelines that determine how much you can deduct:

- How much is the property worth?

- Where is the property in the recovery period? (from purchase to the 27.5-year limit)

- What is the method of depreciation?

Many real estate investors use a method of depreciation called the Modified Accelerated Cost Recovery System (MACRS).

Other Benefits

When it comes to tax advantages for real estate investors, there are many, and too many to cover in depth here; like the 1031 exchange and the self-employment tax and how structuring your business can profoundly impact the benefits you can take advantage of.

What you need to know is this: consult a CPA who is experienced in dealing with real estate investors. He will be able to help you navigate all of the jargon and nuance, and ultimately, help you reap all of the rewards available to you. Don't go into tax season thinking you can do it all on your own. Get a professional to help you out. Trust us, it will be one of the best decisions you make!

Tax Traps to Watch Out For

Before we move on from taxes, a few quick words of warning. Even though the tax breaks are big for real estate investors, there are also some major ways you can find yourself in trouble. Usually, they happen because investors misunderstand and don't take the time to clarify how tax laws work.

Earlier, we talked about using maintenance as tax write-offs. And you can. You can't, however, use improvements—anything that adds value to your property rather than maintaining it—as tax write-offs. Improvements, renovations, and remodeling are all out except through depreciation.

Know going in that if you decide to shell out a few thousand dollars for renovations, you likely aren't going to be able to write it off in your taxes.

Unless you showed positive passive income in the eyes of the government, you might have trouble writing off passive activity (which real estate investment is, according to the IRS) deductions thanks to the passive loss limitation.

If you broke even or showed losses, you won't get to see tax deductions annually—not until you have positive income, or when you sell the property. There are a few loopholes to this: one being if your adjusted gross income is below $100,000. Then, you can write off up to $25,000 in passive losses. Up to $150,000, you can write off a percentage of the $25,000.

For more information, see Publication 925 at www.irs.gov and consult with your tax preparation professional. That is the best advice I can give you when it comes to taxes and the intricacies of building your portfolio. For each of us, how we are able to properly file our taxes and take advantage of all of the tax code to make better investment decisions is very important. I have barely scratched the surface here on the tax benefits and the various ways to use the tax code. A quality CPA or other qualified tax professional is an invaluable addition to your team.

THE PATH TO FINANCIAL FREEDOM

When it comes to planning for your retirement, it's been proven time and time again by successful investors that real estate works. Is it a sure thing? No, of course not. Nothing in life is! And everything comes with a risk, this included. But risk is never a reason not to take advantage of the opportunities right in front of you.

But once you're on this path, making money, and deep into investing in real estate, where do you go? What do you do with that money?

The financial trappings of real estate investment can be daunting and complicated. The best advice we can ultimately give is to focus on due diligence: start with a solid financial plan, examine real numbers, and talk to experienced finance and tax professionals. Do the work that prevents careless mistakes.

You will go far in real estate investment if you build a solid foundation!

Avoid mistakes. Start your real estate investing career with the experts on your side.

THE TURNKEY SAFELY CHECKLIST

Financial Planning

🔑 What resources do I have to get started?

🔑 How much money will I need to build my portfolio?

🔑 What are the hard costs that come with owning a turnkey investment property?

1. _____

_____

2. _____

_____

3. _____

_____

4. _____

_____

5. _____

_____

6. _____

_____

TURNKEY MASTERY TIPS

Understand the importance of positive cash flow.

There are two ways that real estate investors receive income on a property, but only one that puts dollars in your pocket. Rental income and appreciation are both very important. However, when you start building your portfolio, make sure you are buying properties that will produce a yearly, positive cash flow. Appreciation comes over time, but making a positive cash flow from the beginning is a powerful motivator to keep building.

CHAPTER 4

THE BASICS OF USING A SELF-DIRECTED IRA TO BUY TURNKEY REAL ESTATE

If you want to be successful as a real estate investor, you have to spend some time understanding the tedious, yet very impactful specifics of how you buy your properties. We just covered a few of the ins and outs of buying property, including how to use financing and some of the specifics that go along with that, how and when to use cash, and closing costs and how you have to specifically plan for exactly how many dollars you need for each deal.

Believe me, I know this is not exciting. How we go about funding our portfolio is not a sexy topic. It is, however, vitally important if you want to build a turnkey portfolio the right way. Having a basic understanding is a requirement, and we should all be willing to spend a little time understanding the basics and even in the more detailed world of creatively financing our portfolio. Using a SDIRA definitely falls in the world of creative financing. Stay with me and let's get through this together so we can get down to business of the steps to building your portfolio!

THE BASICS OF SELF-DIRECTED IRA INVESTING

As real estate investors, we're always looking for opportunities to secure our financial future, to secure our vision. That is the entire point of investing in real estate. We also know that the more we can do passively, using a turnkey company, the faster we can secure that vision. The passive income we gain through our real estate investing is the means we use to provide for our vision and to save up for retirement. But have you thought about using your retirement savings to boost your investments and save more in the long run? With a self-directed IRA, you just may be able to do it.

What is a self-directed IRA?

A self-directed individual retirement account (SDIRA) is a specialized type of Investment Retirement Arrangement that allows holders to invest in a wider pool of opportunities—real estate included—entirely by their own direction. Unlike a regular IRA, you're not constrained to investing in stocks, bonds, and mutual funds. You invest *with* your self-directed IRA rather than money out of your own pocket, and all profits go directly back into your retirement savings. You essentially own your investment properties inside of your IRA, and returns are added back to your account as well.

As with a regular IRA, all contributions to a self-directed IRA are tax deductible. Transactions within the account are also tax-free while in the account: you only have to deal with taxes once you decide to withdraw. If you with withdraw before the age of 59½, you'll be subject to a 10 percent penalty. Otherwise, you'll only then be responsible for federal taxes on the account.

What is allowed?

Self-directed IRAs can be used to diversify your portfolio in real estate, limited partnerships, franchises, private stocks, gold, and more. One of the big advantages of a self-directed IRA is simply in the freedom to invest in more and diversify your portfolio with your IRA account—and only in the investments *you* want to pursue.

Investing in single-family real estate has never been an option for traditional IRA clients, to the best of my knowledge. Yet, as we've already talked about, we want to invest in real estate. With the advent of using self-directed IRAs to build our real estate portfolio, we now have that chance.

That said, there are still restrictions on how your self-directed IRA can be used:

What isn't allowed?

As with traditional IRAs, you can't invest in life insurance benefits or collectibles (such a baseball cards, art, wine, cars, etc.). However, the *big* things that aren't permitted where SDIRAs are concerned have to deal with *you*, and not your investments. You cannot:

- **Self-deal.** "Self-dealing" refers to the IRA owner, lineal family, spouse, or other disqualified person using IRA funds for their direct benefit in the *present*, rather than building up IRA funds for the future. Some examples of self-dealing include:

- You (the IRA owner) live in or work in a property owned by your SDIRA.
- You use SDIRA funds to invest in your own company.
- A family member rents a property owned by your SDIRA.

Who are disqualified persons?

Disqualified persons rules prohibit your SDIRA from directly or indirectly selling, exchanging, or leasing a property; lending money or credit; transferring or using IRA income and/or assets; or funding goods, services, or facilities. While you own your SDIRA, you cannot receive benefits from the account until you collect them at retirement.

Disqualified persons are:

- You, the IRA owner

- Your spouse or children (and their spouses)

- Your parents, grandparents, or great-grandparents

- Grandchildren and great-grandchildren (and their spouses)

Also excluded are services providers of your SDIRA, including the custodian, CPA, and financial planner. Entities (corporations, partnerships, LLCs, trusts, and estates) may also be disqualified if 50 percent or more is owned directly or indirectly by you or a service provider. A partner who holds 10 percent or more in a joint venture in one of these entities is also disqualified.

In general, the IRS defines a prohibited transaction as:

any improper use of your IRA account or annuity by you, your beneficiary or any disqualified person. Disqualified persons include your fiduciary and members of your family (spouse, ancestor, lineal descendant, and any spouse of lineal descendant).

Remember: all SDIRA owners *must* follow all IRS regulations. It is best to consult with your legal and financial professionals.

You may be thinking: Okay, so my SDIRA can't directly benefit me or my family. So, why is it a good option for turnkey real estate investment? The answer is, because it is a passive investment. An SDIRA is tailor-made with its rules for a turnkey portfolio where the investor is a strictly passive investor.

ADVANTAGES OF A SELF-DIRECTED IRA

A self-directed IRA has several advantages for turnkey real estate investment.

It's passive.

Investing in real estate by traditional means is *also* passive, but the differentiation here is that the SDIRA effectively contains your investment funds. You use SDIRA money to fuel your real estate investments, and then the passive income you earn goes right back into the SDIRA—passively building up your retirement funds in one neat place.

It has big tax advantages.

Tax advantages are a big incentive to use a self-directed IRA for your investments. Not only do you enjoy transactions within your account tax-free until retirement, but there are opportunities for tax deductions as well. In addition, *some* self-directed IRAs allow you to pass assets to beneficiaries after death with little to no tax implications, meaning you can help ensure financial security for future generations.

It offers wider investment opportunities.

Again, the biggest advantage of a SDIRA over a traditional IRA is the diversity of your investment options. Obviously, you can invest in real estate, but you can also turn to *other* investments to diversify your portfolio and mitigate risk.

It provides secure retirement funding.

The entire *point* of your self-directed IRA is to provide secure finances for your retirement. But it should also be noted that your SDIRA is protected under federal bankruptcy laws, meaning that your assets stay secure for the future. As far as efficiency in saving for your retirement through investing goes, it doesn't get much better than a self-directed IRA, if only because it remains contained in the account. No, you don't get the advantage of immediate profits, but you work more efficiently to secure your future.

The fact that a SDIRA account is a tremendous tool to be used by turnkey real estate investors should be obvious by now. That does not mean we can all call up a local financial advisor or stock broker and open an account. There are still more rules and regulations to be aware of.

WHAT ACCOUNTS ARE ELIGIBLE?

Does a self-directed IRA sound attractive to you? There's good news: *anyone* is eligible to open a self-directed IRA. You may be wondering . . . if that's the case, why haven't I heard about it before? Why aren't more people taking advantage of a SDIRA?

Truth be told, this type of IRA has largely flown under the radar, but they've been around since traditional IRAs were created in 1974. The IRS has always—*always*—allowed investments that go beyond the traditional stocks, bonds, and mutual funds.

You likely haven't heard of it because most banks and brokerage firms only allow traditional investments. For a self-directed IRA, you'll likely have to specifically seek out an alternative investments firm.

WHO ARE THE MAJOR PLAYERS
IN THE INDUSTRY?

Before we list some of the big names in the alternative investments industry, we should go over the a few definitions, as many companies will vary in structure, and picking what's right for your investment strategy is crucial for an amiable, efficient partnership.

Custodians

These are the most common, and generally what you will want to look for when you wish to own a self-directed IRA. Custodians are either a bank, credit union, or nonbank custodian that has been approved by the IRS, such as a broker-dealer with IRA approval. Custodians are subject to strict oversight, both at the state and federal level. They are *not* advisors, and as such, are not permitted to give tax, legal, or investment advice to their clients. They also can't promote or endorse specific investments or types of investments. They are there to hold your account *only*, until you claim it at retirement.

Third-Party Administrators

Administrators still require an identified custodian for your SDIRA account, but their primary function is administrative. As a role, administrators exist in a similar capacity to custodians (in that they hold your account and do not render advice), but they do ensure that you are following all IRS guidelines and offer guidance through any transactions you choose to take.

Unlike custodians, administrators are *not* approved by the IRS, are not regulated at the state or federal level, and are not allowed to custody assets. Custodians, by contrast, are. Think of administrators (and facilitators) as an intermediary between you, the account holder, and a custodian.

Facilitators

The difference between an administrator and a facilitator is in their core functions. Like administrators, facilitators play by different IRA rules than custodians. They aren't approved or regulated by the IRS either. Functionally, facilitators are there *mostly* to help owners set up single-member LLCs and C Corporation IRAs.

Why does it matter, you may ask?

Because administrators and facilitators are *not* subject to the same oversight as a custodian, you may inadvertently engage in a prohibited transaction that the IRA catches later—which means being slapped with a big fine.

IT'S YOUR RESPONSIBILITY
AT THE END OF THE DAY

The Retirement Industry Trust Association (RITA) is the voice of the self-directed IRA industry. If you visit its web address (http://www.ritaus.org) you can see all of your qualified self-directed IRA options. I have listed some of the big-name players in the world of self-directed IRAs below.

Remember: these are not recommendations or endorsements. I encourage you to research each company carefully before choosing.

Custodians

Equity Trust Company
Kingdom Trust Company
PENSCO
Horizon Trust

Third-Party Administrators and Facilitators

Specialized IRA Services
iPlan Group
uDirect IRA
Next Generation Trust Services
The Entrust Group

HOW DOES A REAL ESTATE
INVESTOR GET STARTED?

This section outlines the first steps in using a SDIRA for your turnkey investments.

Vet a SDIRA company.

While I have provided a good list to get you started in looking for a SDIRA custodian, administrator, or facilitator, doing your homework *before* entrusting your financial future to a company is absolutely crucial. There *are* disreputable companies out there. While it's not impossible to move your funds if you wind up dissatisfied, there may be fees and headaches involved with the process.

So, what are the most crucial qualities in a good SDIRA company?

- **Experience.** Self-directed IRAs may have been around for a while, but companies that actually specialize in them, let alone allow them, are relatively new. In a field with so many legal trappings that could result in financial disaster, knowing that you have an experienced team in your corner is invaluable.

- **Knowledge.** Another facet of experience is *knowledge*. Not only do you hope that your company has years of experience under its belt, but you also want its professionals to be up on current law and industry trends, and generally knowledgeable of their industry. Don't be afraid to dive deep and interrogate them to see if they really know their stuff.

- **Communication.** In the world of investing, things can happen *fast*. You need to know that your transactions will be completed smoothly and quickly, with ample communication in between. If you have trouble reaching your SDIRA company, you may have a problem—or at the very least, more than your share of frustrations.

Open a self-directed account.

Once you've vetted your custodian, administrator, or facilitator, it's time to open an account. That's it. That's step two! *Anyone* can open a self-directed IRA account. The catch only comes if your chosen company has certain minimum investment requirements. Still, there aren't limitations on *who* can open an account.

*Important reminder! What can be self-directed

You are not limited to self-directing traditional and Roth IRAs. For the self-employed individual and those with a multitude of entities there are self-directed SEPs, SIMPLEs, Solo 401(k)s, Roth Solo 401(k)s, and for those with more participants, self-directed safe harbor 401(k)s as well.

Two accounts often overlooked are HSAs, Health Spending Accounts (HSAs), and Coverdell Educational Savings Accounts (CESAs). If you have a high-deductible health plan, you should absolutely have a self-directed HSA. CESAs can be applied not only for higher education, but for K–12 as well.

FUND YOUR ACCOUNT

So, you've set up your SDIRA. Now it's time to get funded. There are two primary ways of doing this:

Roll over funds from a 401(k), other IRA, or retirement account.

If you already have a retirement account in the works, roll it over into your account. This is the easiest way to start *quickly.* Of course, you may not have enough in that account to fund the investments you'd like to. That's why, among other alternatives, you can do the following:

Make annual contributions.

There are, however, limits on annual contributions. These are set by the IRS. For individuals age 50 and under, the limit is $5,500 annually. For those over 50, the limit is $6,500 annually.

There's potential to drastically increase this limit with a Roth Solo 401(k). If you are self-employed, you should look into this account. For individuals 50 and under, the limit is $34,000 tax-deferred and $18,000 tax-free. For those over 50, the limit is $34,000 tax-deferred and $24,000 tax-free. That's over three times the tax-free savings and five times the tax-deferred savings.

INVEST IN REAL ESTATE VIA YOUR IRA

In a regular IRA, your investments are largely picked for you, and very limited. The only common avenue of investing in real estate with an IRA was in buying shares of an REIT. A self-directed IRA means that you're at the reins! Your custodian won't (or shouldn't) steer you toward any particular investment. Custodians only process transactions. You determine what those transactions are.

One key to note is that when you invest in real estate with your SDIRA, *all* funding for the investment must come from your SDIRA. Not your personal bank account. That doesn't *just* mean purchasing the property: it means everything you need to maintain it, repair it, and manage it. It is *vital* that you don't overspend and that you have an ample cushion in your SDIRA.

This is especially important considering the limitations on your annual contributions. You can't necessarily bail your SDIRA out when costs overreach your balance.

In the last chapter I talked about the no big deal fund and the fact that investors need to pay attention to economics and make sure they can afford an investment instead of relying on an account like this to cover all expenses. Remember, this is real estate, and there will be bad days. You just have to be pre-pared so it's no big deal!

However, with an SDIRA, it is very important that an inves-tor not overspend when buying real estate. Make sure that you leave a healthy cushion in your account. If you have $105,000 in your SDIRA, I would not suggest buying a $100,000 property. As an investor, I prefer to use no more than 80 to 85 percent of my investment funds on an investment. Especially real estate! That leaves a healthy balance to handle those rainy days when they come. Bills and expenses must come from the account and cannot come from your personal account.

If, for any reason, you do not have the funds in your account, it is not easy to make deposits. So be careful.

All expenses are paid for by the IRA, not you. All income goes to the IRA, not you. The property is *owned* by the IRA, not you. Keep this separation in mind—it'll prevent you from getting tangled up in legalities.

Note that this means rent checks must be payable to your IRA account, not your name.

WHAT A TRANSACTION LOOKS LIKE

Let's say Investor A, Allen, decides to open a self-directed IRA account, which he decides to fund with his 401(k) from a for-mer employer. Allen wants to invest in real estate with his SDIRA, so he identifies a property that he wants. He speaks to his custodian about making this transaction, and he makes an all-cash bid that is entirely covered by his IRA, and in the name of his IRA account.

Once the bid is accepted and the proper paperwork completed between Allen and his custodians, the property is now owned *by* his SDIRA account. From this point on, all expenses, including property taxes, property management, and maintenance, will be covered by his SDIRA account. Income will funnel back into the account, tax-free, thus building up his retirement funds.

Of course, Allen was lucky: he had enough money in his account to cover his transaction. But what do you do if your IRA doesn't have enough funds to cover the costs of purchasing, managing, and maintaining your investment property?

WHAT IF I DON'T HAVE ENOUGH IN MY IRA TO COVER AN INVESTMENT PURCHASE?

You're not totally out of luck. Outside of making your annual contributions to the account, you can:

Transfer from another IRA or qualified plan.

Do you have another traditional IRA or retirement plan? If qualified, you can roll these funds over into your SDIRA. Consolidating these funds might seem like putting all of your eggs in one basket, but remember: a big advantage in a self-directed IRA is that ability to diversify your portfolio on *your terms* and mitigate risk.

Borrow money (nonrecourse loans only).

Because you cannot be personally responsible to pay for a loan associated with your SDIRA, only nonrecourse loans (in which the property is the collateral) are acceptable to help with funding through your self-directed IRA.

Partner up.

Partnerships, even with disqualified persons, are possible for the initial purchase of an asset. While this may seem like it's breaking the rules, it isn't: the stipulation is that you or a disqualified person does not already own the property. You can go in and purchase a portion using IRA funds, in the name of your account, while a partner (including friends or family) fund the rest. Expenses and income are divided proportionally to your share of the asset.

When and if you sell the property, your account will receive a percentage that matches your initial contribution.

Sell another asset.

Finally, you can sell assets that are already owned by your self-directed IRA account: these funds will go right back into your account, meaning you can pay attention to appreciation and earn more than you paid at purchase.

DETAILS EVERY INVESTOR SHOULD KNOW BEFORE GETTING STARTED

I can't pretend that a self-directed IRA is a foolproof way to invest. Far from it: it can be an extremely risky endeavor, despite nice tax advantages and bankruptcy protection. Before you jump into real estate investment through your SDIRA, be aware of some of the potential pitfalls:

Risk of Fraud

The U.S. Securities and Exchange Commission (SEC) warns investors of the different kinds of fraud that can exploit the self-directed IRA system. Ponzi schemes and fraud are no less common here than elsewhere. Remember, too: not all custodians, administrators, and facilitators are created equal. Some companies will be better than others in terms of communication and experience, and a lack of either can be detrimental to you.

Know the warning signs of fraud.

Be aware, and watch out for warning signs of fraud.

Unsolicited Investment Offers

Remember: this is a *self-directed* IRA. You are in charge of what you invest in. Whether it's a random promoter or a custodian subtly trying to steer you toward a particular investment, remember: they are not supposed to direct your investments or offer advice. Be wary of *any* unsolicited investment offer, no matter who it's coming from.

Guaranteed Returns

As always, be on the lookout for any offer that sounds too good to be true. Astronomical return projections or promises of returns are big red flags as always.

Ask Questions

Whether it's the company managing your SDIRA account or an investment promoter, *ask questions*. Don't be afraid to dig deep and hit hard. Make sure all licensing is up to snuff and that all numbers are checked out and verified.

IT CAN BE HIGH-RISK

While the freedom to direct your own investments is one of the major perks of a SDIRA account, it also comes with the obvious dangers that *any* investment does. Self-directed IRAs are suited for experienced investors with a proven track record of success, and not for those who are hinging their entire retirement or economic future on an IRA.

Because of the restrictions placed on annual financial contributions to your IRA, you only have so much room for error.

A few bad deals can easily wipe out your entire account if you're not careful. That said, if you as an investor do your due diligence and make wise investment decisions, you're not likely to run into catastrophe. But it's worth repeating that being too cavalier with your SDIRA investments is a bad, bad idea.

Despite the risks, however, a skilled investor has a lot to gain from a self-directed IRA. They're best suited for investors looking to passively secure their financial future, while also wanting a hand in what those investments are. For real estate investors, the opportunity is real.

Now that you have a better understanding of using leverage and the basics of using your retirement accounts to super-boost your retirement, we have to get serious about researching how to buy turnkey real estate. In the next chapter, I'll take you through the first part of that process: researching the market.

THE TURNKEY SAFELY CHECKLIST

Using a Self-Directed IRA to Buy Turnkey Real Estate

- Do you have an IRA that you can convert or an SDIRA already set up?

- How much is in your IRA accounts?

- What are you allowed to invest in with your SDIRA?

- What is disqualified for you as an investment with your SDIRA?

- What are the most crucial qualities in a good SDIRA company?

  1. _____

  _____

  2. _____

  _____

  3. _____

  _____

- What are two warning signs of fraud when investing your SDIRA?

  1. _____

  _____

  2. _____

  _____

TURNKEY MASTERY TIPS

Don't forget to include your retirement accounts or a retirement account strategy as part of your plan for reaching your vision.

Most real estate investors that I work with build their vision around using their cash and finding a way to leverage into multiple properties. It is only after a little digging on my part that they realize they have an IRA account that they can use as well. A big part of every investor's vision is retirement. How great would it be to own your portfolio inside your IRA and receive the rent payments during retirement tax-deferred or even tax-free?

RESEARCH THE MARKET

"**Y**es, hello, listen. I'm on your company website, and I see you have eight properties for sale in Memphis. I want to buy all of them."

The man on the other end of the line was someone I'd never spoken to before. He introduced himself as Jack, a businessman from Chicago. He'd visited Memphis once before and taken a shine to it, so he wanted to invest here. But after a few minutes of conversation, it became clear to me that that was the extent of his research on the local market—a fact that didn't slow him down. "I'm ready to invest today," he said. "Shoot me over some contracts."

I didn't feel right selling Jack all eight properties at once, under the circumstances. "Look," I told him, "Here's what we can do. I'll sell you one or two of these properties to start so you can get a feel for our company and this market. If everything works out, then great. You can buy more houses from there."

A beat of silence went by on the other end of the line. I could hear him take in a deep breath like he was trying to compose himself, and he started into why he didn't need to go slow. He had done his research. He was a very successful businessperson.

He knew how to make deals and knew that real estate was exactly what he wanted to invest in.

He had heard all about Memphis as a great investment market and was very proud of the fact that he knew he could find "great, cheap deals" in the market. What he really needed was someone who could manage everything for him.

At the time, our company was pretty big. We were buying, renovating, selling, and managing close to 200 properties a year. The turnkey real estate industry was still relatively new, but our company was one of the first to concentrate on building our brand. We had built several avenues through advertising, use of a blog, publishing educational articles, and doing podcasts that were all meant to build our brand. It was apparent to me that Jack had heard about our company and decided he wanted to get going right away.

The problem at the time was that the more I dug, the clearer it became that Jack was in too much of a hurry. He hadn't done his research. Regardless of what he knew about me, he had no clear vision for why he wanted to invest in real estate and knew little to nothing about the market. He was shooting from the hip.

We spent half an hour on the phone with me trying to direct the conversation toward his getting educated on why Memphis might be the right market for him and him trying to steer the conversation back to buying eight properties on the spot. When it became apparent that I wasn't going to sell him the eight properties I had available, he said something that I have never forgotten.

"Mr. Clothier," Jack said finally, "you are the worst salesman I have ever spoken to in my life." When I stuck to my guns, he added, "You will regret your decision," and hung up. A week later, he called back to tell me again how bad a salesperson I was. He couldn't wait to tell me he'd bought 12 properties in Memphis from another company. I laugh thinking back now how proud he was that he bought 12 properties. Not eight like what I had, but he had actually bought even more.

I knew the company that he had bought from and the areas that it managed. Needless to say, we weren't doing business in the same parts of town. I just shook my head and wished him the best of luck.

Later, I learned that Jack had paid market premium for 12 poor-quality houses in an area of town where rents were falling due to the neighborhoods being older, dilapidated, and economically challenged. To say these houses were located in struggling areas would be an understatement.

Now, I'm not saying that an investor shouldn't invest in a struggling neighborhood or take on the challenge of bringing some renewal and change to neighborhoods that are neglected. I am saying that it is almost impossible for that to happen with a turnkey company. Those properties and those neighborhoods that are in struggling areas of cities need local investors. They need a concerted effort from a lot of groups including local investors. Exactly how that looks is another topic for another time. I will discuss a little later the details of why low-cost properties in struggling neighborhoods simply do not make economic sense for a turnkey investor. In a nutshell, there is too much risk.

Jack is a perfect example, as you will see, of why that risk is made much worse by investors who are in too much of a hurry to investigate where they are investing. His unstable tenants didn't stay in the properties long. The properties were never properly renovated, which left residents frustrated and moving out quickly, which led to vacancy, lost rents, and vandalism and left him with thousands of dollars in repair bills every time they vacated.

A year later, Jack called me again. This time, he wanted to know if we would buy those 12 substandard properties from him. He was ready to make a deal and offload them quick and at a substantial loss.

"Jack," I said "I'm sorry, but you were in too much of a hurry to know what you were buying. You didn't research the market. You didn't care about the neighborhoods you were buying. You didn't even want to take the time to learn how a company manages properties and how it tries to hold down vacancies and maintenance. You were in too much of a hurry to take time to understand what you were buying. You just wanted in. I can't take those houses off your hands. They simply are not in areas that I would buy for my portfolio, much less want to manage, so I won't buy them for my clients, either." Again, I wished him the best of luck.

Jack ended up selling most of those properties at a tremendous loss—all because he couldn't be bothered to research the market before he invested.

THE VALUE OF RESEARCH

The beautiful thing about the turnkey revolution is that you can invest in turnkey real estate from anywhere. If you follow the steps laid out in this book, you can literally invest anywhere in the world. But, as Jack learned the hard way, you need to do your due diligence on the market beforehand if you expect to invest wisely. That means understanding from a big level all the way down to the details you are going to rely on your turnkey partner to know. You don't need to know the details of every neighborhood. You just need to know that your partner does and that it is not willing to compromise your investments to make money.

Some people say that the first thing you need to research when you're thinking about investing in turnkey is your team. But in the Turnkey Safely System, "who" comes second. The first thing you really want to figure out is "where": Which markets are right for you?

Not all markets are created equal. That's why there's no substitute for doing research before you invest. When you take the time to do this step right, you will end up with a list of strong cities to consider and explore for quality turnkey companies. Taken with the steps that follow, you will only review houses that meet your expectations from companies that meet your expectations in cities that meet your expectations. You will build a portfolio that will continue to prosper over time, effectively growing your investment. If you don't, you risk ending up like Jack, saddled with terrible investments that push your goals out of reach.

Researching a market correctly means that you arrive at a decision based on facts, not emotions. You never choose a market because you visited the city once and liked it, or because your college roommate lives there. If you have a neighbor or family member that has invested in a city and she loves it, fantastic. Put it on your list to investigate. If, for some reason, you just really love the idea or thought of investing in a city, put it on your list, but if the data says don't invest, you don't invest. No matter how many times someone else tells you how great his investments are or how much he loves the city.

If you make a decision based on emotion, you risk investing in a shrinking or dying market. And that will ultimately compromise your vision.

Each year, new investment opportunities pop up in every city. But how do you determine which ones offer you a better return on your investment? What information should you be looking for? And even after you've determined that a handful of markets look like safe bets, how do you further narrow down your list?

The information you need to weed out the bad markets from the good ones is out there. You just have to know where to find it. In this second step of the Turnkey Safely System, I'll teach you how to research potential markets so that you can make the right investment decisions for yourself and your family.

HOW TO RESEARCH THE MARKET: THE RESEARCH FUNNEL

Researching the market is a process that starts with a wide list of cities you're interested in, and then narrows as you eliminate markets that are unsafe prospects for you. At Memphis Invest, we call this process the research funnel (see figure).

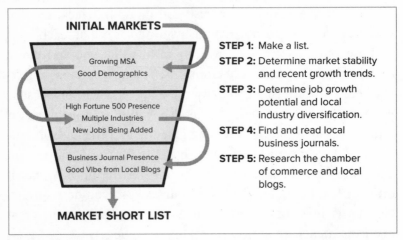

The research funnel

By the time you complete this process, you will have the one, two, or three cities that offer the best opportunities and biggest returns for your specific needs. The five steps of the research funnel are making a list, determining market stability and growth trends, determining job growth and industry diversification, reading local business journals, and researching the chamber of commerce and local blogs.

Step 1: Make a list.

At the top of the research funnel, you cast a wide net. Step 1 is where you make your list of all the markets you want to research.

The chances are good that you already have some idea of where you're interested in investing. Regardless of how that list was put together, you have it and you need to commit it to paper. When you put your list together, don't stop at the cities you have in mind right now. Think bigger. Where else might be a good prospective market for you?

You can actually lay out a map when you're doing this and ask yourself, "What cities have I heard about that are good places to live and work? What are the big cities? What are the medium-size ones? What's going on in Dallas? Is it shrinking or growing? How about Kansas City, or Cleveland, Ohio? How about Houston, or Oklahoma City, or even Memphis? What's happening with those cities?"

Write down each city that catches your eye, and take some time to think about what you know about it. What about each of them interests you? Again, this list will be made up of cities you have included for many reasons. Just because you were told it was a good investment city or because you liked visiting, it doesn't mean it is actually a good investment city. This is the step where we find that out. For now, include everything.

The more cities you research, the more options you have, and the better chance you have of finding a market or markets that are a perfect fit for you. Think of the world as your oyster during this step. Really take your time and look and don't count anything out just yet.

Step 2: Determine market stability and recent growth trends.

Once you have your list, you need to go city by city for the rest of the research process. Step 2 is to determine the market stability and recent growth trends of the different cities on your list.

The first thing to look at for each city is the key indicator of its stability in recent years: its population. What has been happening with its population growth over the last 10, 15, and 20 years?

The best place to look for this information is the Census Bureau. Specifically, you want the last two censuses taken for that city and its metro statistical area (MSA). You're looking for at least a break-even number in population growth. Even if an MSA has shrunk a little bit, there may be enough stability still there that the city is on its way to recovering. But you don't want to buy investment property in a city that's half the size it was in 1995.

The reason I look at both city and MSA data is that many cities are experiencing suburban growth around them, while the city centers and areas within city limits are not growing. Revitalizing dilapidated city centers is a huge focus for many cities, and attracting population growth inside city limits is difficult. So, it is important to look at the entire metro area to get a clearer picture of what's happening with population.

Population isn't the only indicator of stability in a city, as I'll cover in a moment, and in some cases a recent population drop can actually be an opportunity to buy while prices are low and likely to rise again in the near future. If that seems to be the case, you've found a good reason to keep that city on the list.

You're not going to cut out a lot of cities based on population growth alone. Instead, use it to get a feel for an area. Then continue to build a full picture of what's going on in that market. Remember, population statistics only tell a tiny part of the picture. You are really determining that a city is not on a long losing streak that will be hard to come back from.

Step 3: Determine job growth potential and local industry diversification.

After you have an idea of population growth trends in the market you're researching, the next question to ask is, "What's happening with this city's economic growth, and how is that affecting this market's stability?"

The single most important factor in determining the economic stability and growth potential for a city is its industry. The number one reason people leave an MSA is that there are no jobs there. Lack of growth and vitality leave a city without a pulse. The lack of energy and diversification in the job market leaves a big hole for a city that is tough to fill. Therefore, you ideally want to invest in a market that is highly diversified.

Dallas is a great example of diversification. A huge percentage of jobs in Dallas are provided by almost two dozen different industries. There are 22 different companies from the Fortune 500 headquartered in Dallas. Those industries are so diverse (and growing) that any downturn in one or two of them hardly causes a ripple in the job market. If one of those industries—say oil, or airlines—is experiencing difficulties, there are still plenty of other opportunities to be found there. That is incredible diversification.

By contrast, some cities will have a single dominant industry providing jobs. In those markets, it's important to know what that industry is and what the projections of its long-term stability look like.

Industry strength is an important factor. We found several years ago, in the first decade of the twenty-first century, the importance of not building city or even a region's employment on the back of one industry and the ancillary industries that supply it. When the economic crisis hit in 2007, the auto industry ground to a halt.

American auto giants like Ford, Chrysler, and Chevrolet found themselves in an industry under siege. As the demand for new cars plummeted, so did the need for workers, production, plants, and offices. Thousands of workers lost their jobs. Not only the auto workers, but also the parts suppliers, the distributors, mechanics, steel workers, parts suppliers, and on and on and on. Down the list it went, and more and more workers lost their jobs.

Entire cities across the rust belt were decimated and faced a rebuilding effort without the advantage of job and industry diversification. These cities faced a crisis like they had never seen before, and to this day, not all of those cities have been able to bounce back.

Contrast that with another city that relies heavily on one industry. A city like Memphis is built on multiple different industries and has been diversifying for the past decade. However, one industry still dominates. Memphis is and always will be the transportation and distribution capital of America. If something ships, it probably touches Memphis at some point.

The difference between industries like transportation and distribution and the auto industry is that as long as America is producing goods, they will need to be shipped, warehoused, and distributed. The transportation industry will always be in demand and is one of the first industries to rebound after a downturn. As production begins to ramp up, the distribution model kicks in. That is a healthy industry that is going to be in demand regardless of market conditions.

How a city is going to fare in a downturn and how diversified or strong the industries providing jobs are is a tough call to project. That is why I caution that it is a small piece of your puzzle. It is a piece, though, and it is important. I would not suggest investing in a city that really lacks potential for growth.

Your best resource for researching the potential for job growth in a target city is Google. For example, if you want to know about job growth in Cleveland, just type "job growth Cleveland" into the search bar and read what comes up. The research and opinion has already been done for you. It is out there, you just need to spend some time finding it and reading.

Another good query to use is "net job growth" paired with the city name you're researching. This will give you a picture of what's really going on with employment in that area. What companies are moving in? Who is providing jobs? What industries are they in? The reason you want to check "net job growth" is that the rosy side of the picture is often painted brilliantly. You'll find lots of hoopla about job growth. Finding out about job losses takes a bit more digging, and the net job growth figure takes both into account. A city may be adding jobs, but if it is losing jobs at the same rate, there won't be much job growth. Make sure you dig for the whole picture.

Understanding job growth and industries goes a long way toward identifying stable markets. But you're not done with the research funnel yet.

Step 4: Find and read local business journals.

The fourth step in the research funnel is to find and read a prospective city's business journals. I prefer to invest in a city that is large enough to have a business journal presence, because that means there's business, growth, and enough local industry to support and drive that level of local engagement. There are 43 different business journal publications, which provide a pretty diverse number of cities to investigate. That does not mean a city without one should be off your list. Oklahoma City does not have a business journal, and I am very excited about investing in Oklahoma City. But, the presence of a business journal is one of my key indicators of future growth and stability.

Go to Google and type in the city name along with "business journal." If one or more business journals come up, you're in good shape.

Once you've found your business journals, read them. What businesses and industries are making news here? Is there a story about one major local company whose stock is falling and that is laying off 50 percent of its workforce? These are things you need to know before you invest there, not after. A business journal exists in a city for one reason: to produce news stories about a city's businesses and industries. Its journalists are going to be connected and get the word out quick on both the good and the bad. Local business leaders love reading them and rely on them for early indications of what is happening and to get the full behind-the-scenes details of the health of a city's business climate. They are important.

Reading the city's business journal gives you a sense of the local business climate. If everything still looks good at this point, you're in good shape. There's only one more test to pass in the research funnel.

Step 5: Research the chamber of commerce and local blogs.

The fifth step is to research the city's chamber of commerce and local blogs. Any city that has made it this far in the research funnel very likely offers a safe, attractive market. But you may still have more markets on the list than you care to buy into. This step in the process is a way to narrow it down to the absolute cream of the crop.

Visit Google again, and this time look up the city's chamber of commerce. When you find its site, download and read any brochures listed there.

When you do this, you have to keep in mind that this brochure is full of information viewed through rose-colored glasses. It's going to be the rosiest, brightest version of the area you can get. There will be another side to the story of business and life in that city. Nevertheless, it's the job of that chamber of commerce to know and market the selling points of doing business in that city. And that's valuable information to you as a potential investor in the area. I want to get that picture of a city.

I also want to get the other side. You can find the unvarnished truth about doing business in a city by reading local blogs. These don't even all have to be business blogs. They might be about food, or the schools, or the arts, or parks and recreation—all sorts of topics related to working and living in that city.

Reading local blogs doesn't take long, and what you get out of it is an insider's unfiltered view of a city. If there is dirt to be dished on a place, this is where you'll find it. And that information is just as important in getting a balanced view of the local market as the polished marketing copy put out by the chamber of commerce.

Right now, you may already be thinking to yourself, "This is going to take forever!" This should be a quick exercise and not a dive down a rabbit hole. You are skimming across the top and just digging in below the surface. You do not need to know the facts for population growth for every year, and you're not trying to determine migration patterns or determine exactly which jobs are being created and what the wages are. Those are in-depth questions that get answered later, and they get answered by the experts you are working with in your chosen market or markets.

You are spending maybe an hour or a little more on each market and quickly getting a feel for which markets need to be on your short list. You are eliminating the markets that don't give you a good feel and highlighting those that do. That is all you are doing at this stage. Just because you highlight a city on your list does not mean you are going to invest in that city. There is still work to do. So, don't get bogged down and don't get discouraged thinking you are going to be spending hours and hours on research for each city.

You are simply narrowing your choices!

SHOULD I VISIT THE MARKET?

"Should I visit the market?" is a big question when it comes to turnkey.

The answer is no, you don't need to at this point. You may want to at a future date, but right now put off the idea of traveling to the city. You can safely buy real estate without ever laying eyes on it as long as you know the facts. Instead, you visit the market for confirmation after you've chosen it and decided on your turnkey team.

The reason you want to do it this way is that you don't know what you don't know. If you go to a market before you have a team, you don't know what you're looking at. You have no clue. Some people try to do super detailed research. "This is the best zip code based on the best school rating and the crime reports," they decide, and they start driving through neighborhoods. When they get there, they think, "All of this looks really good. Yeah, I want to buy here. This is the neighborhood I want to buy in."

But they don't have a team in place. They don't know what the locals know: that that street of houses is actually bad because the shoulder is split down the middle of the road. They don't know the little things that make houses stand out or not stand out to people who live in the area. They lack the knowledge that a local provider is going to have. The knowledge that says from this point north the homes are good, but south on this same street is less desirable.

It is the difference between success and failure as an investor, and visiting a city without knowing what you are looking at only adds to confusion. Don't be that investor.

Cities are going to look extremely similar on the surface. Knowing the subtext is what matters. You don't need to drive yourself around a strange city, figuring out where the crime is and where the good schools are. That's not your job.

Your job is to trust the research you did on the market—and the reliable team that you ultimately hope to find to work with you there. That comes next in the process. The best thing you can do as a passive investor is inform yourself on the markets you like, make your list, and move to the next step of the process. There will be a time for visiting a market when you are ready to meet a team.

AN INFORMED MARKET DECISION

At the end of the day, a house is a house. But a city is not just a city. You need to know the stability and economics of a local market before you decide to invest there.

The five steps of the research funnel may sound like a lot of work, but they're not. You don't have to write a 20-page thesis on each city. A couple hours here and there is all it really takes to do this right. Check your facts and jot down some notes. At most, you should be spending just a couple of nights per city.

None of the five steps of the research funnel is enough, on its own, to say yes or no to a market. But all of them taken together will present you with a full picture of what's going on in that city and help you answer the question, "Is this place a good investment city for me?"

Determining which markets are good and safe simplifies your decision process and paves the way for your personal turnkey revolution to take place. Don't make the mistake of investing in a market you haven't investigated and vetted. No matter how you have initially built your list—if you added cities because you visited them or your best friend or boss has an investment property there—you must arm yourself with the facts and stay informed.

At this point in the Turnkey Safely System, you've learned how to use the research funnel to weed out unsafe markets and identify the best of the best. You know *where* you want to invest, but you can't do it alone. In the next chapter, I'll teach you everything you need to know about how to choose the right team to manage your turnkey investment.

THE TURNKEY SAFELY CHECKLIST

Researching the Market

🔑 Have I put in a lot of time and effort to research markets of interest to me?

🔑 Does this market I'm interested in have strong population stability and economic growth potential?

🔑 Does this market have a local business journal?

🔑 What have I learned about this market from reading the local business journal, chamber of commerce brochure, and local blogs?

🔑 Taking all of this under consideration, does this market pass the research funnel test?

TURNKEY MASTERY TIPS

Make decisions based on facts—*not* feelings.

Just being familiar with a market is not what I consider "digging deep" in your market research. Make sure you don't decide to invest in a market because you are already familiar with it and really like the market. That is not enough. Always do thorough research, and follow the facts!

You do not have to visit a market before you choose to invest.

I get asked quite often if I think visiting markets is important. You do not have to visit a market before you choose to invest. Visiting the market is a step you take to build your rapport with your chosen turnkey partner, and that may happen before or after you have chosen to get started investing, depending upon the circumstances.

CHOOSE YOUR TURNKEY COMPANY

Jean and Sofia had immigrated to the United States from Europe—and as passive real estate investors, they had been through every turnkey nightmare under the sun. No one they worked with had been reliable, so they had received unexpected cash calls on multiple occasions. They had replaced roofs, plumbing, and appliances, and sometimes they were replacing these items over and over. Tenants had moved out on them in the middle of the night. They'd purchased "super-cheap" properties in multiple cities across the country from different companies and individuals. These properties and the lack of a plan had cost them an arm and a leg to this point.

They made a slight adjustment to their plan and started purchasing more expensive properties, thinking the cheap price point was the issue. There again, they were wrong. It wasn't the price point that was the issue. It was their choice of teams to work with in the different markets that was causing their nightmare.

Once a property of theirs was damaged by a tornado, and they didn't know about it for two whole months. By the time their management company sent someone out to collect rent, the tenants were gone and the house was gathering dust. A lack of communication and failure to manage expectations was seriously draining their bank account as well as their enthusiasm for passive real estate investing.

Yet in spite of all that, they knew that turnkey real estate was still the right investment for them. They just had to find a partner responsible enough to make it work the way they knew it should.

As Sofia tells the story, she had attended real estate investor association events and had somehow ended up on the mailing list of a real estate magazine based in California. She had never paid much attention to it, but one particular issue had the words "turnkey real estate" on the cover, and it caught her attention. She read the articles and saw an announcement for a talk I was giving in Los Angeles, where they lived, called "How to Safely Buy Turnkey."

She attended the event. She liked what she heard.

Two weeks later, she and Jean were sitting in my office in Memphis. We took our time, and I worked through their goals and investments with them. For the first time, the speech they heard wasn't "buy, buy, buy." It was "investigate, learn, get to know us, make sure we're a good fit."

Jean and Sofia knew that they were finally hearing what they needed to hear, and they didn't mess around. A week later, they bought five properties from us. Things went so well that, eventually, they sold all their other investments and bought more houses from our company instead. Then they referred other members of their family to do the same thing.

A few years later, several generations of their family were investing in turnkey headache free, and they were well on their way to achieving their visions.

TURNKEY MASTERY TIP

If it feels like a sales pitch, it's a sales pitch.

I can't emphasize enough how important it is that whomever you do business with takes the time to get to know you on the front end. Not just what your vision is and how your goals help you get there, but really getting to know if the company is a good fit for you. Pay attention early on to the questions team members ask and the direction they lead the conversation. If it feels like a sales pitch, then it's a sales pitch.

As we go through this chapter and I show you how to find a great turnkey company to work with, this tip is important. Make the company earn your business by going slow. Be patient as an investor and make the company's people spend time with you. There are many companies that want to move quick because their business model requires it. If customers took their time getting to know them and their properties, they would never sell a thing. So they have to rely on urgency and scarcity to make you think that you have to move now or you will miss out. Scratch those companies right off your list!

YOUR TEAM: THE "KEY" IN TURNKEY

Before they found us, Jean and Sofia were not investing in turnkey. They were just buying houses from people and companies who didn't know how to manage them. The properties were in pretty good markets overall, but that may have been more luck than anything. Jean and Sofia had made a big mistake at the beginning. They were investing in cheap properties—cheap by their standards because they lived in California—and not paying enough attention to the market or who they were doing business with.

That's not turnkey—that's a headache. And it's also the reason that the team you choose to work with is what really puts the "key" in turnkey real estate.

A true turnkey partner is a real estate company that purchases an investment property, renovates that property to a high level of quality, places a tenant in the house, manages the occupied property—and only then sells it to you, the investor, as a performing asset. There really is no other definition that works if you are going to buy a turnkey property.

The problem is that *turnkey* has become a marketing term. It hasn't been mainstream long enough for people to have clear standards for it. Anybody out there can say, "I'm a turnkey company." But the reality is that some of these companies may not own their maintenance services. In some instances, they don't even own the houses they sell you. They just don't do the things that need to be done to protect the investor.

A quality turnkey company will own everything it sells, and the renovations will be completed on each property before it is marketed to an investor. Anything short of that brings risk. Anything short of that is not really turnkey. You should never be asked to pay for renovations after you purchase a property. That's not turnkey. That's a recipe for getting ripped off. And yet there are companies that use the word *turnkey* to market their properties, and they ask investors to buy the property and then pay for the renovation while it's being completed. That is simply too much risk.

Don't let that deter you though. That doesn't mean you shouldn't invest in turnkey. What it means is that you need to do a great job choosing an outstanding turnkey partner before you invest.

A bad turnkey company can destroy a great investment. If you don't take the time to handle this part of the process right, you stand to lose every dollar that you put into your venture. Worse, a bad turnkey experience can derail the vision of where you want to go. However, if you make the effort to sort through the false advertising and find a high-quality turnkey partner, the path to your vision will be much smoother than you thought it would be—and you'll reach your goals much more quickly.

When you invest in turnkey real estate, you have to be confident in the company you choose to work with. You have researched the city and know the facts, but the company you work with is intimately familiar with the city. Its staff members have a deeper understanding, down to the subtleties of which side of the street to own a property on in a particular neighborhood. Those are the details you don't need to know—but your turnkey partner does!

Choosing your turnkey partner is a critical part of the turnkey revolution, and the third step in the Turnkey Safely System. This chapter will give you a complete system for how to find and screen top-notch turnkey companies so you can invest in passive real estate with clarity and confidence.

HOW TO CHOOSE YOUR TURNKEY PARTNER

Choosing an ideal turnkey company is a three-part process. You need to identify good options, put your finalists to the Turnkey Test™, and take stock of the investments they offer to see if they're a match for you.

Identify good options.

The first part of the process is identifying good options. This is where you learn what's out there and strain the false advertising from the companies with real potential. Start with a simple Google search. Using the target markets you identified in the last chapter, type each city name plus "turnkey real estate" into the search bar. You can also try queries like "best turnkey real estate companies" and "largest turnkey real estate companies" for your target city. Then, take a look at the results that come up.

If nothing pops up at all, that's not a good sign. It doesn't necessarily mean that turnkey companies don't exist in that area, but it does mean that they are probably not big enough to do business with. Companies that have the technology to keep you happy as an investor from 1,500 miles away almost always have a strong Internet presence.

Ideally, you want to see two or three turnkey companies when you do this search. That's a sign that there's some traction in the market. There's a demand for the service in the first place. At that point, you do some basic due diligence.

Your goal here is just to identify the big players and strain out the mosquitoes. Don't worry about the details of the company itself and how it's run yet. Figure out who's big enough to investigate further. Who appears multiple times in the search results? Who has a high-quality website? These are some early warning signs. You know off the bat that you don't want to do business with a company that has a three-page website with no pictures on it. Forget the companies that use an obvious template with no mention of ownership, leadership team, the structure of the company, or their personal story.

On the other hand, when you find a company that turns up in 80 percent of the search results, has a well-done website, is quoted in major periodicals and newspapers, and is clearly active with things such as articles, videos, and press releases, you've hit on an option that has some meat on its bones. These are the companies that go on your short list to do more research on.

This stage of the process is also where you keep whittling down the two or three market options you found in the last chapter. If you get to the end of this step and you don't see a company with potential in your target city, scratch that city off your list. It doesn't matter how good the market itself looks. Without good turnkey company options, you don't want to invest there, plain and simple.

Put your finalists to the Turnkey Test

Online presence is a start, but does it mean a turnkey company is up to scratch? No. Unfortunately, an online presence is not enough to say a company is quality. Many companies today are getting better and better at perfecting their marketing. It is slick, it is smooth, and what with turnkey's growing popularity, there's more and more of it out there. Since we know that not having an online presence is a deal killer, how do we separate the good from the bad? After you've narrowed your options down to a few finalists, you need to put them through a much more intense screening process to figure out who will be the best partner for you in the end.

I call this screening process the Turnkey Test. This is where you separate the people who have real companies from the people who are just selling houses.

How do you get started?

First, reach out to the company. From this alone, you will probably be able to tell whether you're dealing with low, mid-level, or high quality. A low-level company will respond to your request for more information with something like "Sign up to get a list of all our houses sent to you." Sometimes, low-level companies fail to respond at all.

The next step up from that is a company that gives you something closer to "Here's a free report about how to invest in turnkey safely." These are usually "stay small, keep it all" kinds of companies. You might get the impression that they're not bad, when you talk to them, but they're not quite as sharp and 100 percent on top of things as you'd like them to be.

The worst of the low-tier and middle-tier companies are the ones that have well-oiled sales machines that use the best of the psychological sales techniques to fool an investor. They may tell you that you have to wait for five to six weeks before you can get an appointment to speak with someone because they are "so backlogged with demand." This gives the impression that the company must be exceptionally good if there is so much demand.

Another technique is to respond that you can have an appointment, but you need to be prepared to move quickly on the call and commit to properties immediately. Even waiting one hour can be enough to cause you to lose a property. This use of urgency and high pressure is a way of social-proofing their company and making you think that everyone else is investing and making fast decisions, so you need to as well.

I'm not saying that companies may not have high demand or packed schedules. I'm not saying that companies may not sell properties very quickly. What I am cautioning you as an investor to watch out for is the companies that are not interested in getting to know you. They are not interested in more than a few minutes of an introductory call and some cursory questions before they get right into selling you properties. Look for companies that make you feel comfortable and are obviously confident in their value. They will spend as much time as you need without any feeling of pressure.

The top-tier companies will offer you a full welcome package explaining how to get started with them. The extra time they spend and the effort they put into educating you as an investor on their company and their process will go a long way in building the trust you need to buy from across the country or world. The difference will be obvious and well worth the effort, and so will the results.

However, just because a company's team members spend time talking with you and don't rush straight into trying to sell properties doesn't necessarily mean it's the right fit for you. Top-tier companies are more likely to have the manpower and experience to handle your investment with the most service and the lowest risk.

Whatever the case, request a conversation with the turnkey companies you find. Just say, "I need to get some details about your company. Can we spend 30 minutes on the phone?" If they tell you no, that's a red flag to cross them off your list. If they say yes, you get on the phone and ask them this series of questions—the Turnkey Test:

TURNKEY TEST

Are you an investor?
Very important question. What you want to hear is that the company itself is indeed an investor. If companies are not investors themselves, move on. If they are, find out how long they have been investing. If the answer is that they started investing after the 2007 housing crash, that should raise some concern. That would mean they have been investing while the market has been improving. They have been building a company or their services during a tremendous growing market. They may not have the expertise to know how to protect you during a housing downturn. This is not a

deal killer, but certainly the longer the company has been in operation, the better for you as an investor. You would typically like to see a little grey hair on the company!

Do you own in the exact neighborhoods you are selling?

Assuming they say yes, they are an investor, you get to the next question. It is important that they invest alongside their clients. They need to own in the same neighborhoods that they sell. Don't settle for a simple yes. Really dig in here and ask why they choose the neighborhoods they choose and how invested are they.

How many investors do you work with?

Simple question. You are looking to see how big the company is. You can use this information later in the test to determine how many properties each investor owns on average.

Do you own all facets of the operation?

This is very important. I would caution you to only do business with companies that physically own the properties they are selling and own the renovation company as well as the property management company. If they own all services of your turnkey investment, then there is only one number to call when there is an issue. If a company tells you that it sticks to finding and selling and then introduces you to its partner companies who renovate and manage, move on. This is a disaster scenario. If there is an issue, you will end up with multiple companies pointing the finger at each other and no one taking responsibility to help you as an investor. Stick with one company that offers all the services.

Do you offer rental or maintenance guarantees?

If they answer yes, ask them why. Then ask them if they will put the guarantee on year three. Guarantees are used by some turnkey companies as a sales gimmick and should be a red flag for an investor. (I'll discuss this more later in the chapter.) They are selling the guarantee rather than a quality service and product. Usually the guarantee is a one-year promise that you will have no maintenance costs and no vacancies. The problem is, if you are working with a quality company, there shouldn't be maintenance or vacancy in the first year. Instead, companies raise the price of a property and cut back on the work they do. They gamble that in the first year, they can cover whatever maintenance issues come up, and they can keep a tenant in a property long enough to last the guaranteed first year. When year two hits, the costs fall on the owner of the property. If you like the idea of a company guaranteeing to cover maintenance and vacancy for a year, ask them to put the guarantee on year three when you should expect to have some issues. If they are willing to make that kind of guarantee, then you may have found a quality turkey company. That is the only way I would be interested in a guarantee as an investor.

Do you defer maintenance?

Most companies will have no idea what you are talking about. So, clear it up for them by asking if they fix and/

or replace everything on the house. Do they protect you as an investor by limiting your maintenance costs? Or do they defer maintenance such as leaving a roof on because it looks like it has a few years left? Do they choose to fix rather than replace a water heater that is on its last legs because an investor can get a year or two out of it? Do they fill up the AC unit with Freon because it is cheaper than replacing the whole unit? Each of these scenarios lowers your entry cost as an investor, but raises your holding costs by raising the amount of money you will spend each year fixing and maintaining your property. It will cost you money in the long run. I estimate that an investor will pay between $2 and $3 for every $1 in renovation that is skipped on the front end.

How many properties do you manage?
Simply put, the larger the portfolio under management, the higher the likelihood companies will have systems in place to provide excellent service. Smaller companies simply do not have the manpower and processes in place that it takes to keep your passive investment portfolio running smoothly. You are not looking for a cheap property management solution here. The larger management companies can sometimes have a larger price tag, but that price should translate to better service and communication.

Do you own the properties you sell?
It should be a given at this point. If companies are simply selling properties from the MLS or representing properties from other investors, they are not the right

company. They need to have a vested interest in the property themselves. If they are not willing to put their money on the line and buy the properties first and complete the renovations before selling, then you are taking all the risk in the investment. If they can't afford to buy the houses, then they haven't been in business long enough nor been successful enough for you to trust them with your portfolio. Stick with the companies that know how to operate. They buy the properties that they like, that they want to manage. They renovate them and then offer their properties to other investors.

How long have you been in the business?
I've already covered why this is so important, but you need to ask the question directly. "How many years have you been in the turnkey real estate business?" So many companies pop up every year. You have to be careful as an investor and look past marketing and smooth sales talk. Experience matters in this business, and this is your money. I often ask audiences if they have ever experienced the holdup in a Jetway while trying to board an airplane. I explain to them that if they are flying with my dad, they are going to experience this delay. He is the type that wants to stop by the cockpit and peek his head inside to say hello. He always says he is looking for a little grey hair up there flying his plane. He likes to know that the pilot has a few years flying under his belt and would have experienced a lot of different scenarios that may come up while in the air. It makes him feel better at 40,000 feet! The same goes for you when investing in real estate. Look for a little experience. In this business, longevity is a good thing.

What is your average vacancy rate?

This is a very typical question to ask a company that manages property—a basic. Remember, if a company does not manage the investments itself and instead chooses to have you work with an outside management company, it is not a true turnkey provider and you are asking for trouble. Make note of the company's answer and put it off to the side. You are going to ask the same question from the opposite direction in a minute and compare the two answers. Honesty is way more important right now than simply having a good answer.

What percentage of expiring leases will renew their lease each month?

Why does this matter? As an investor, you want to work with a company that values the experience you have owning your portfolio. This is an investment, and you should expect a consistent and reliable experience. Vacancy and turnover are not pleasant experiences, although they are a part of owning real estate. A company that can limit the number of vacancies you have and increase the length of time a property is occupied is a company working in your best interest. A company that doesn't even bother to track this figure is not worth spending much more time talking with.

What percentage of signed leases fulfill their full term?

Same concept with this question. Is the company focusing on keeping its residents happy? Happy residents are going to stay longer in a property. They are going to treat the property better and have a better relationship with the management company. This number is a sign of how good the management side of the turnkey company is at doing their number one job—keeping your properties occupied and paying rent.

What is the average number of days a property is vacant between tenants, move-out to move-in?
This is another one of the basics—the questions you have to ask and write down their numbers. Good companies are going to track this kind of data. They will be on top of their numbers. Great companies are going to track this data and explain to you in detail how their systems, team, and operations work to improve these numbers. Pay attention to the details, and don't hesitate to ask them how their performance stacks up to other companies and if they are satisfied that their performance is as good as it can be.

What percentage of billed rent do you collect each month?
This is a tricky question, and you may not find many companies in your search who track this data accurately. That does not mean they won't have an answer, but if you hear 100 percent, then you need to move on. They are either not big enough, haven't been in business long enough, or are lying with that answer. Contrast the answer with the answer they gave on how many signed leases reach full term, and you can see if they are giving you accurate information. Late payments are a part of a business and make up a percentage of rent payments each month. So are nonpayments and move-outs. Those things happen in this business. It is

unlikely that you will ever find a company that collects 100 percent of every rent bill each month.

What is the cost of an average repair bill after move-out?

Another basic question. However, what you are really listening for here is how well the company renovates its homes and treats the residents. A home without deferred maintenance will not require high repair costs after move-out. Residents that are treated with respect will treat the property with respect. Will there be repair costs at every move-out? Absolutely. But a well-run management company that really understands how to manage both the property and relationships will help hold down your costs.

What are your management fees?

Another fairly straightforward and basic question. You are looking for a company with a simple, easy-to-understand pricing structure. It makes money when you make money. It should be easy to understand and a handful of charges at the most. That means two to four revenue streams that you pay for as an investor. What you want to avoid is a company with a whole buffet of charges where you are paying for every single thing the company does. That is a recipe for confusion, and as an investor, you should expect better from a management company.

What percentage of collected rent goes to yearly maintenance on average?

With this question, you're trying to find out how good the company is at holding down maintenance costs while the property is occupied. The lower the percentage the better, obviously, but don't just write this down and move on. This is an important question, and it is going to help us later on. We will use it in our final analysis and when we interview current clients.

What is your average number of months occupancy per property?

What you are looking for here is how long a resident stays in a property. If a company says it has a high number of completed leases and a high number of leases that extend and resign for an extended period, then this number too should reflect that. As an example, the company should be able to tell you that the average length of occupancy is 33 months or something to that effect. Just write down the answer, and I promise that you will have enough to build a clear picture of whether this a company you would want to partner with or not.

We are not quite done with our Turnkey Test yet. The following three questions are critical. Beyond our first list, here are the three most important questions you can ask to learn a little about your potential company's mindset as business owners and how they are going to treat your investments:

What programs do you have in place to keep residents happy?

Remember when you asked the average number of leases that go to completion? Remember when you asked how many months a property stays occupied? Remember the question about maintenance and move-out costs? This is where you hold a company accountable to its answers. What is the company doing to keep residents happy? Does it have financial literacy or education classes? Does it offer services to help residents qualify to purchase a property? Does it get involved with community service that directly affects its residents? Those would all be excellent answers, but listen for the basics. This is where so many turnkey companies fail. Do team members answer the phone when their residents have a problem? Do they call their residents back after a maintenance issue to make sure they are completely satisfied with the work? Are they tracking the number of maintenance issues a resident has within 30 days of move-in to assess how good their renovation teams are performing before they hand over the keys? The real test to see if a company is top-notch is how it treats its residents. These are the people after all who will directly determine the success of your investment.

What customer service programs do you have in place? Will you call me every month with an update on my portfolio? How many team members are dedicated solely to providing service to your clients?

How about you as a client—would you like to feel special as an investor and receive outstanding customer service? The days of accepting poor property management are over. If you are buying a turnkey property, it should be a must, or you should move on! Do not accept mediocre management and being made to feel like you are a passive investor only who should sit back and collect checks. That is not how this works. The best of the best will have programs in place to contact you as an investor monthly or at a minimum on a very regular basis. Team members should be dedicated to staying in constant contact so you feel updated and comfortable with your investment. Ask how they provide these services and if they have team members solely dedicated to your communication and satisfaction.

What has been your biggest mistake as an investor? How do you protect your clients from making the same mistakes?
Way back in the opening of the book I told you that I had made just about every mistake you can make as a real estate investor. I have made some pretty dumb decisions. I don't say that as something I am proud of, but I'm not embarrassed, either. It is part of my journey as a real estate investor and ultimately as an entrepreneur helping other investors. If someone can't come up with a really good mistake he has made, not a mistake that costs a few bucks here or there, but something that could be catastrophic for other investors, then I'm not sure I would trust that person as a turnkey provider. Why? It goes back to the whole grey hair thing and how long a company has been in business. Investors who came through the last housing

crash came out bruised and a little bloody. Those were the lucky ones. Most came out beaten up and barely moving if they survived the crash to begin with.

I cannot stress enough that you want to do business with people who understand what it feels like to lose. They know what it feels like to have evictions and maintenance and no communication from your management company. They know exactly how they *don't* want you to feel. More importantly, they are willing to own up to it and explain how they design their company, team, and processes to protect you from the same mistakes.

If the company's answers to the Turnkey Test are satisfactory, that's a great sign that you're dealing with trustworthy, responsible people who know what they're doing. But you still have one more thing to discuss with them before you sign on: the housing itself.

Take stock of their stock.

Just because a company passes the Turnkey Test doesn't mean it will have the right kinds of investments for you. This is where you communicate your vision and goals to your potential turnkey partner and see if they match what the company has to offer.

At this stage, a good turnkey team will turn the tables and begin to interview you instead. Team members will ask what you're looking for specifically, and why you want what you want. Then they'll help you find a way to meet your goals if they can.

For example, you could say, "I love duplexes, and I only want to invest in those." A good company might reply, "You know, we don't do duplexes because they're in the wrong part of town. But tell me why you only want duplexes." If you can achieve your goal with single-family homes just as well as duplexes in that particular city, the company will let you know, and you might keep that company on your list as a possible company to move forward with after all.

What is more likely to happen at this point is a discussion about age of the houses and types of neighborhoods. A common way to score properties is to assign them a letter grade. Homes may be assigned a grade of "A," which implies that these are excellent assets where most if not all of the homes are of high retail quality and the homes in the neighborhood will be mostly filled with owner-occupants.

There will not be a lot of rental properties in these neighborhoods, and those that do exist will tend to be more expensive. While that may sound like a negative since the higher they are priced, the more it costs to invest and the harder it is to see a positive return, these properties also tend to have the best opportunity for appreciation and fewer turnovers. Residents tend to stay longer.

Next come the "B" properties, which tend to be nicer homes, newer neighborhoods, above median home value for an area, and while there are rental properties in these neighborhoods, most homes will tend to be owned by owner-occupants. These make really good turnkey rental properties.

Properties that are rated "C" and "D" you want be cautious with as a turnkey investor, and to be direct, stay away from the "D" properties altogether. Houses that are rated so poorly are in bad neighborhoods and work best for active investors managing their own portfolios.

I am not a fan of labeling properties with the "A, B, C, D" method, but it is a common practice. You will run into it as you are interviewing turnkey companies. As an investor, remember that the method is very subjective, and what rates as a "B" property in a "B" neighborhood to a company selling a property may be very different from what an investor trying to add a property to her portfolio would consider a "B" property.

If in the discussion it becomes apparent that a company is not able to offer what you need for your portfolio, then you're looking for a good referral or a point in the right direction. It could be that the company's price points are too high. Possibly it specializes in one type of property and you are comfortable with another. It could be the company simply doesn't spend enough time and attention on the renovation. Either way, this is your portfolio, and the properties themselves need to match your needs.

If you can't afford an investment with the company you like, but you can afford a less expensive one with a questionable company, don't buy either one of them. The former costs too much, but the latter delivers no value. Just keep looking for another place to do business. This alone can save you thousands of dollars in bad decisions.

When a high-quality company's properties match your needs, then it's safe to sign on with your new turnkey partner. You don't need to meet the team in person first, though you can do that later for confirmation if you want to. As long as you follow this process correctly, by the time you reach this point, you shouldn't have anything to worry about.

You're in good hands.

DON'T BUY CHEAP HOUSES

Yes, I am back to this point. Why? Because it is the one rule you should never break when investing in turnkey: don't buy cheap houses.

Turnkey is not the kind of investment you should ever make by searching for the cheapest option. When you choose a turnkey vendor, the price point of the homes it sells reflects the value of what you're getting.

Why?

Because there's a lot more to good property management than putting up a sign in a yard, taking a phone call, showing a house to somebody, and collecting the rent. Turnkey companies that stop there are giving you a lower level of service, connectivity, and satisfaction. These are companies that often sell houses for less than $50,000 and charge a 5 or 6 percent fee on the rent collected. They tend to cut corners that put you at risk as an investor.

Meanwhile, good turnkey companies have a high level of two things: service and renovation work. They don't sell bad properties that have issues. They don't delay work that needs to be done right away, and they don't go cheap on their value. You can expect a good turnkey company to charge between 9 and 10 percent of the rent, and you can expect it to be able to tell you why.

The reality is that your property manager is the factor that makes or breaks your success. When you're looking at potential turnkey companies, remember: more expensive doesn't always mean better, but cheaper almost always means worse.

SHINY OBJECT SYNDROME (S.O.S.)

The biggest trap that investors fall into when searching for turnkey companies is what I like to call Shiny Object Syndrome. Shiny Object Syndrome refers to the marketing gimmicks companies throw at you that don't have any added value—in particular, guarantees.

I'm a big opponent of guarantees. In my years of experience, guarantees are offered for only one reason: to attract the buyer. It doesn't matter how a company frames it. Luring you in is the bottom line. Two of the most common guarantees are that you will not miss rent or pay any maintenance costs for the first 12 months.

But if you're working with a quality turnkey company, you shouldn't have to deal with vacancy or maintenance in the first year, period. That should never happen. And if it does, the company shouldn't charge it to the investor anyway, because that company failed. A really high-quality turnkey company that knows it's the best can prove it to you without gimmicks such as guarantees.

If the idea of a guarantee appeals to you, I suggest you tell that company that you want the guarantee the third year instead of the first 12 months. See if it's good enough to stand by its product that far down the road as much as it will in years one and two. The last thing you want is to buy a bunch of properties in year one under the protection of a guarantee and then be stuck with investments that perform terribly every year after that.

Shiny Object Syndrome doesn't stay shiny for long. It will have you sending out an S.O.S. before you know it.

THE VALUE OF GOOD PEOPLE

Benjamin Graham, investor and mentor to Warren Buffet, once said, "Price is what you pay. Value is what you get." This is absolutely true of turnkey companies.

What matters at the end of the day is the value you're getting for every dollar that you put into your investment. That's where the payoff comes from. That's where the ability to achieve your vision really comes into play. And that's why the team you choose is so much more important than everything else in the turnkey revolution.

The value of a good turnkey company is immeasurable. It will give you a level of comfort and peace in an investment that you're making thousands of miles away. Once you've found a partner that's a good fit for you, you're ready to move forward to the next step in the Turnkey Safely System.

Now it's time to create your plan.

THE TURNKEY SAFELY CHECKLIST

Choosing Your Turnkey Company

🔑 Are there any turnkey companies available in my target city?

🔑 Does my potential turnkey company have a strong online presence?

🔑 Am I satisfied with my potential company's answers to the Turnkey Test?

🔑 Does my potential company offer stock that meets my investing needs?

🔑 Am I signing on with my company based on value instead of price?

TURNKEY MASTERY TIPS

Avoid Shiny Object Syndrome.

Shiny Object Syndrome is best described as that pit in your stomach that seems to almost always form right after making a big buying decision. It asks if we got the best deal or if we negotiated hard enough. It is the nagging thought that there is always something better than the deal I got or a price lower than the one I am paying. Fight the urge! If you have done your homework and know exactly how an investment fits into your goals and drives you toward your vision, then make the investment.

How do I define value?

I measure the value of my investments by how much money they make relative to how convenient they are for me, and how relatively secure. The return I get has very little to do with the actual value equation I use. It's a reflection of the value I attribute to convenience and security.

CREATE A PLAN FOR YOUR TURNKEY INVESTMENTS

The previous chapter discussed the questions you need to ask a turnkey company in the Turnkey Test. The last question was super important. You wanted to know if the company was humble. If it had been in business long enough to make enough mistakes to protect you, and were team members willing to share those experiences? More importantly, were they willing to set up a company with systems, processes, and a team all designed to protect you from making the same mistakes? Well, had you asked me that question, here would be my answer:

IN OVER MY HEAD

I was living in Colorado with my wife and our first child when the first company I had started on my own began to grow. It was generating enough extra money for me to begin investing in my family's future. I had a vision for what I wanted that future to look like, but I knew that wasn't enough. I needed a way to get there.

So, I made a plan. My goal was to buy enough properties to fund my retirement and provide a legacy for my children. My investment properties would pay for college and weddings, and I wanted to give each of my kids a house for graduation or as a wedding present. Could you imagine any better gift to give your kids at the start of their life as a family than an investment property free and clear?

More than anything, I wanted to give my kids something other than money. I wanted to give them an example of hard work and smart planning. Owning 15 properties free and clear was what it would take to achieve this, so that became my plan: acquire and pay off 15 properties.

I had fantastic connections in Memphis: my family. All of us were investing in single-family homes at the same time, and my dad was building processes to manage the properties. I trusted my family members and knew that they would help me achieve my vision.

Armed with this plan, I went out and invested. In the beginning, I made some good investment decisions, and along with those good decisions came a little bit of monthly income. I also made a few bad decisions, and with those bad decisions came a little less monthly income, even monthly losses. Over time, I got the hang of things and began to focus more and more on real estate.

I started buying properties with less and less due diligence. I started looking at riskier and riskier investments, because I thought I was the X factor. I was making good decisions, which was leading to more money, and my mind began doing bigger and bigger math. I quit focusing on fundamentals and trusting my partners who were managing the properties and started adding properties I was finding on my own.

By not doing proper due diligence and venturing further from what had helped me build a small and performing portfolio, I began to grow my portfolio faster and was adding greater and greater risk without knowing it. I was no longer following my plan. Little did I know that my vision of owning 15 properties free and clear was getting further and further away.

One day, I looked up and realized that I owned 57 properties.

Now, let me put this in perspective a bit. I didn't own these properties free and clear. I had purchased them and put notes against them. To say I was overleveraged is a bit of an understatement. No one I was speaking with was advising me to do differently. Who knows if I would have listened, but money was easy to find, and I was all about buying real estate. I may have been borderline addicted at this point. I even purchased 11 houses in one day—and they all had interest-only loans against them. I was convinced that appreciation was where the future was headed.

The turning point for me occurred one Monday night when I sat down at my home office desk after working all day at my regular office and faced over 100 pieces of mail. Insurance notices, tax notices, monthly statements, bills to be paid. I was exhausted and for the first time became scared. What had I done? In four short years, I had destroyed what should have been a slam dunk.

I realized that I'd thrown my plan out the window. In doing that, I had created an unsustainable business cycle for myself. I was in way over my head, buried under the sheer amount of paperwork required to keep up with all those properties.

And then the 2007 real estate bubble burst.

Before I finish, I want you to understand *exactly* what the biggest mistake was that I have ever made as a real estate investor. I failed to follow my plan. Period!

I wanted to own 15 properties free and clear, and that was my plan. I didn't need 57 properties. I began to listen to the wrong people giving me lots of advice on using no-money-down strategies and how equity and refinancing were the way to build real wealth. On paper, I was already a millionaire.

My mistake was letting other people turn my plan into their plan.

Overloaded with so many properties, I spent two years working hard and losing sleep trying to unload as many of them as possible. I took steep losses every month but found a way to stay current on all of the bills. After two years, I made the decision to try to work with lenders. All of the local banks were thankful that I sat down with them and worked out a restructuring plan. I was not as fortunate with the national banks and had several refuse to work with me. It was a difficult time, but I battled for several years to work out my problem properties.

If I had just followed my plan, I could have saved myself a mountain of money and headache. It took me five years to recover from that market crash. Today, I have a good-looking, safe, and high-performing portfolio. I'm back on track with my original plan. And I've never looked back.

A PLAN FOR SUCCESS

You've seen that laying out your vision, researching the market, and finding the right turnkey team are all key elements of successfully participating in the turnkey revolution. But if you don't have a solid investment plan or don't bother to follow the plan you have, you can still find yourself in hot water like I did.

Having a plan and sticking with it is important. It is the layout of your goals and the pathway to your vision. Your plan ties the two together. Without the plan, how will you know if you are actually moving toward your vision? How will you know if you are moving in the right direction? Without that plan to guide you along the way, it's easy to get sidetracked.

If that happens and you run too far off-course, you could find yourself like me—buried under mountains of paperwork, dealing with growing pressure, and having to fight to stay afloat, or worse . . . you could lose everything. Your plan is the map that shows you how to get from where you are now to where you want to be financially 10, 15, or 20 years from now. It's also the benchmark you'll use to measure your success.

Without a plan in place, you will not know if you're on the right course with your investments. You may have good investments, or you may have bad ones—but you won't know which is which if you have no way to track the progress you're making.

The benefit of having a plan is that you understand not only exactly where you want to go, but also what it will take to get there. By sticking with that plan and referring back to it regularly to measure your progress, you'll be well on your way to success.

In this step of the Turnkey Safely System, I'll teach you how to make a turnkey investment plan that's right for you and use it to steer yourself toward the financial future you envision.

MAKE YOUR PLAN

The first thing to know about making your turnkey investment plan is that this is not something you should do on your own.

By now, you've identified at least one turnkey company that you'll be working with to build your passive turnkey portfolio. This is the company that you are trusting as your partner to assist you with hitting your vision and staying accountable to your goals. You'll need to schedule a call or sit down one-on-one with the company in order to make your investment plan. When you combine your clear vision of what you want to achieve and the company's practical experience in the market, you've got a recipe for a successful plan.

I touched on this first step of the process in the last chapter. Your partner's job is to advise you about what kinds of properties offer the right kind of income to fit your needs. At the outset, you may think you need 30 duplexes to achieve your goals, when really 15 newly built single-family homes in your target market offer a better return with fewer headaches.

If you try to create your plan without the company's help, you might end up with those 30 duplexes and a plan headed toward total derailment. Your team's combined knowledge is a great resource for which there is no substitute. It's up to you to make use of the team's expertise.

Once you're sitting down to work on the plan, your partner's team members should ask you a more in-depth series of questions about your goals than they did before, when you were figuring out if the company had the types of investments you needed in general. It's important to communicate honestly and directly with your partner about this so that they can help you create a customized investment plan that's truly right for you.

It may seem a bit unnatural at first, but you really have to open up with your partner about your assets and your abilities. You have to be aware of what your current account balances are and what monies you have to use for down payments on your properties. You need to be aware of your current credit score and what your credit situation looks like. Do you have retirement account monies as we discussed in Chapter 4 that could be used to build your portfolio? Are you self-employed, or have you recently started a new job? Are you planning on leaving your job in the near future?

Self-awareness and an ability and willingness to be open and honest will really help your turnkey partner to build a solid plan with you. Team members will be able to give you advice on how to best structure your investments and how to best reach your goals. Mostly, they will be able to help direct your plan so you actually hit your goals and create your vision.

Your turnkey partner will look at your goals and ask for the reasons behind them. Why do you want to do this? What's motivating your investment goals, and what plans have you already set in motion to achieve them? Have you already set up college funds for your kids, or some other form of generational gifting? Are you putting money away into a retirement plan each month?

It may be that you're starting from scratch on all of these things, and that's fine too. What's important at this stage is for you to be able to give the company a clear picture of your financial goals and where you are now in relation to achieving them.

This conversation lays the groundwork for building not only a successful investment plan but also a true partnership. The company needs to know that it is a great fit for you, and you need to make sure it is the right fit. If the partner you've chosen has sounded great to this point, but for some reason team members are not showing a lot of interest in your goals, path, vision, and ultimately success, then reevaluate. Make sure you are comfortable that your partner is truly a partner.

ASSESS YOUR RISK THRESHOLD

The second part of creating an investment plan with your team is to assess how you feel about risk. This is an important aspect of making any kind of investment plan, and it's no different when it comes to turnkey. Specifically, determining your risk threshold will inform you about what kinds of properties you should consider buying and to what extent you should diversify your portfolio.

Your risk tolerance also plays a role in how you purchase your properties. How much leverage are you comfortable with? How much value do you place in communication with your partner? This is a great time to get really comfortable with how you are going to feel owning real estate investment properties far from where you live. If you sense any hesitation right now, discuss it with your partner. Your turnkey partner needs to help make a plan that gives you comfort when you sleep at night.

To gain an understanding of your comfort zone when it comes to risk, your turnkey partner will ask you another series of specific questions tailored in this direction. These will include things like: How do you feel about vacancies? How do you feel about move-outs, repairs after move-outs, and ongoing maintenance repairs while tenants are in residence? How do you feel about logging into an online portal to view the performance of your portfolio? How do you feel about having a property management team that makes a majority of the active decisions on your properties?

The reason your partner will ask these things is that some of the different categories of homes you can invest in may have greater potential returns but come with a higher level of risk. At the same time, as an investor, it may sound great to buy turnkey real estate, and you may think you are all in, but a really good company is going to uncover your questions and help you find the answers. If there is going to be an issue with the passivity of investing with a turnkey partner, a great company is going to guide you in another direction. There is no point in finding out later on that you really like the active side of investing and being passive is just too uncomfortable. Knowing how comfortable you are with what kind and what level of risk allows the company to make more streamlined recommendations for your investment plan.

LOOKING AT THE FULL PICTURE

For example, a single-family home that's more than 40 years old is probably cheaper to buy than a brand-new home of the same size in the same neighborhood. At first glance, the older home looks like a better return on your investment. But for a fuller picture, you also have to look at the level of rehab and upkeep required for both houses and the risk entailed there.

The more expensive house is brand new, which means no or low rehab costs, and a lower risk of having to pay for repairs. Conversely, the older house may require significant rehab and is going to come with a higher level of risk related to repairs. Plus, due to changing building code regulations, the materials originally used in the older house may also require special handling to dispose of during any necessary repairs.

Another thing to consider is that the company you're working with may have expertise in handling specific types of properties that mitigates a lot of that potential risk on your end. Some management companies, for instance, specialize in taking on older homes and renovating them from top to bottom. In this case, they may be able to do this more cost effectively, passing greater savings and less risk on to you, the investor.

Some companies actually specialize in building brand-new homes from the ground up. They buy infill lots from builders finishing neighborhoods and build new homes. These are then sold to passive investors as turnkey properties and managed by the management company. Again, these are two different scenarios and likely bringing slightly different returns, but each will attract a different investor with different risk tolerances.

In the first half of your conversation about making a plan, your job is to clearly and directly explain your goals and where you are in relation to them to the company. During this second half of the conversation, your job is to honestly and directly explain what kind of risk and how much of it you're comfortable with.

Once you've discussed all of this with the company, it should be able to help you put together a custom-tailored investment plan that meets your goals. This plan should also take into consideration your current level of financial planning, your level of comfort with specific kinds of risk, and the level of portfolio diversification that will best help you achieve your goals based on the assessment of your risk threshold.

You'll likely need to work with your turnkey partner to tweak the plan until it's just right. But if you've checked all of these talking points off the list during the planning process, it will show in the end product: a customized investment plan that will map the road ahead for you, leading you to the financial future you envision.

DIVERSIFY YOUR INVESTMENTS

A good turnkey company will also talk to you about including diversification in your plan. The more properties your plan includes, the more you should consider diversifying as an investor, to protect yourself as much as you can. You can and should diversify within any given city. You can also diversify in different cities.

Some turnkey companies offer properties in multiple cities to begin with. If that's the case, they can offer you that diversification solution. If your turnkey company is limited to one city, however, the next question you want to ask is, "Who else would you recommend I work with in another city?" That really shouldn't be that big of a question, but like always, you are looking for signs that you are with the right company.

Diversification is a big deal. As I stated, you can diversify with different properties spread out through different neighborhoods in one city. There is nothing wrong with taking that route. But you may also want to further diversify by looking at other markets. If the answer you get is pushback that you need to only be doing business with the company you are on the phone with, dig a little further. Surely, if it has your best interest at heart and can't help you diversify into multiple cities, then it can help you find another turnkey partner. It is your plan after all.

One important tip to remember: the more you grow as a turnkey investor, and the more cities you invest in, the more you lower your risk. By spreading your portfolio through multiple markets, you are reducing the risk to your portfolio of a market downturn. Having more than one turnkey partner may not sound ideal, but I would argue that it is better than buying all of your properties in one market only. Just something to keep in mind.

STICK WITH IT

Once you have your investment plan in place, the most important thing to do is simple: stick with it.

One way to make sure you stay on track is to get into a regular routine of reviewing your perfect day and your plan as often as needed so that you don't lose sight of the bigger picture. Don't delegate your responsibility here. This is *your* plan for *your* future. And it's the best tool you have to help keep yourself on track to reach your financial goals.

The moment you lose sight of your plan, you become vulnerable to bad impulse-buy investment decisions. Someone from another company—not *your* management company, because the team there will know better—might call you up out of the blue and say, "Hey, we've got this great deal, and I think it would fit perfectly into your portfolio. Are you interested?" You will absolutely get solicited—by phone, by mail, by email—to buy the "great investment properties" from other companies. I know this to be true because it is exactly how I first fell down the rabbit hole as an investor.

If you've lost sight of your plan, you might say, "Sure," when really, this particular property may be everything you initially set out to avoid in your investment plan—and for good reason.

Instead, when you get that call, it's time to pull out your business plan. Does this new opportunity represent another step toward your goals in your existing plan? Does it fit with your plan for diversification? Ask, "Does this company that solicited me out of the blue even fit the ideals of what I am looking for in a turnkey partner? For that matter, is this even a turnkey opportunity?" If the answer to those questions is yes, it may be something to consider. If the answer is no, you've just saved yourself time, money, and headache, all simply by referring back to your plan.

And remember, sticking with your plan does not mean treating it like it's set in stone. It may be that your long-term financial goals change over time. This is not a reason to chuck your plan out the window. But it may be reason enough to review and revise your plan from time to time.

Based on your actual investment experience, you may look at your plan and realize you're making more than you expected from your investment, or less. If you're making less than you expected, that doesn't necessarily mean it's time to adjust your plan. It just means it's time to continue acquiring more assets until you hit your target income.

If you're making more money than you planned for, that's another story. If your investments are performing better than you expected, and you're comfortable with your active and passive incomes, you may have additional money there that you're able to do something more with. If you're interested in applying that extra income to your long-term turnkey investment plan, now is the time to pull out your plan and make some adjustments to take advantage of that.

The bottom line is that your plan is what keeps you from buying a property just because it's cheap, or because it looks like it offers good returns, or because the properties you already own are giving you a good return. None of these is a reason to go out and buy a new property. The only reason to buy an investment property is because it fits your needs and your plan. Period.

Making a plan to fit your needs and goals and then sticking to it is the key to successful turnkey investing.

CELEBRATE THE SMALL WINS

Here is that concept again. I am a big proponent of living in the moment. I had the opportunity to meet Turney Duff, former Wall Street highflier and author of the book *The Buy Side*, and hear him speak, and he said something that I love. He said he tries to live with his head where his feet are. In that exact moment and at that exact place.

Living in the moment while regularly reviewing your plan allows you to touch back to your vision and become more aware of all that you've accomplished so far. Don't just celebrate the big win at the end, when you've reached your long-term financial goals. Celebrate the small wins each step along the way. Celebrate exactly where you are in that moment, and never forget to keep your head where your feet are. It will help you to navigate those no big deal days.

As your portfolio grows, you're going to start to be able to see your vision become reality as your plan comes to fruition. The line of credit your bank gave you that's going to help you buy your next investment property—that's a win! So, do something to celebrate it. Mark the occasion in whatever small way feels special to you.

You will look up and realize that every lease you have on your properties has been renewed and you can expect another year of no vacancy—that's a win! Celebrate it with a favorite bottle of wine or a dinner with your favorite person.

Your celebration could be something as simple as taking half a day off of work to take the kids to the park. Or maybe you and your spouse like to eat out, but you've been skipping dessert for the past six months to put that money toward the next step in your plan: saving up the money to buy your next property. Once you have that money saved up and you're ready to start looking at houses, it's time to celebrate. Order dessert.

You have a vision of where you want to go, and each step you take toward that vision should be celebrated—especially the small ones. Celebrating your wins will help you keep sight of your larger goal and how far you've come toward it.

You're doing all of these things because you want a bigger and better future for yourself and your family. The sense of accomplishment and pride you'll feel at having made progress toward that future will help you stay motivated to make necessary sacrifices now in the name of your future financial freedom.

Now you've learned how to make a successful investment plan and stick with it. In the next chapter, I'll teach you the next step of the Turnkey Safely System: how to make your investments.

THE TURNKEY SAFELY CHECKLIST

Creating an Investment Plan

- Did I sit down with my team to create an investment plan, or have I been trying to do it all by myself?

- How many properties do I need to include in my portfolio to reach my vision?

- What is my time frame for purchasing these properties?

- Does my plan take into consideration . . .
  - My long-term financial goals?
  - The steps I've taken so far toward meeting those financial goals?
  - What kind of risk I'm comfortable with, and how much?
  - The level of portfolio diversification that will work best for me?

TURNKEY MASTERY TIPS

Review your plan often to make sure you stay on target.

One of the best tips I can give you is to keep your plan close by and make a habit of reviewing it monthly. For most of you, there will be other investments, savings accounts, or income streams that all play a role in your plan. Keeping an eye on your progress will build your enthusiasm, and celebrating even the small wins will keep you inspired to stay on track.

Celebrate small wins.

"When was the last time I celebrated a small win on the path to my long-term financial goals?" Write this question down as part of your plan. Each time you review your plan you'll be looking for the small wins and making sure you celebrate your steady path toward reaching your goals.

MAKE YOUR INVESTMENT

Sam was a super-sharp investor out of San Francisco with a clear plan. He wanted to invest in five turnkey properties in Memphis that would give him consistent income. Sam was entrenched in the high-tech world of Silicon Valley, but he wanted out. He was married with two children, but real estate was his true passion, and he was searching for a way to transition into real estate full-time. Sam followed the path I have laid out so far with one important adjustment.

He bought his first property from us in 2011 at almost retail value for $85,000. Everything went well, and Sam enjoyed working with our team. At the same time as he was purchasing his property, Sam was also attending his local real estate investors club and learning about actively investing in real estate. Other companies were marketing themselves to him. "We can sell you Memphis properties at lower prices," they promised, and eventually Sam altered the execution of his plan.

He bought his second and third properties with two different companies. On paper, the properties were less expensive (they were cheap properties) and the returns they promised looked very promising. The properties themselves fit into his plan, and the companies had very slick marketing. To Sam, it looked like he was making sound decisions.

Then Sam purchased two more properties on his own, spending a lot of time and effort building a team to help him manage his properties remotely on his own. He reasoned that with the discounted prices he could get buying and hiring directly, he could earn a better return. Again, on paper, his investments looked great.

Sam made all five of his investments in 2011. Then in 2014, he came to Memphis to visit his properties, and he came to our offices for a chance to sit down and meet once again.

"I bought five properties in Memphis," he said. "One of them was the most expensive—yours. And that expensive property is the one that gives me the best return to this day."

The other four properties Sam bought were cheaper at first, but their profitability fluctuated up and down constantly. He struggled to get good communication with his other management companies and found remote management didn't translate into real savings. Without the ability to negotiate savings based on volume and face-to-face interaction, Sam had ended up paying more than he anticipated for everything.

Meanwhile, the investment he made with us was steady. In four years, he managed to break even with the other four investment properties. With Memphis Invest, Sam earned a consistent return.

Sam had a great plan for his turnkey investments. But the way he made those investments was not the best strategy for him in the long term. In the end, he had spent greater effort for less return.

The great thing about Sam's story is that he still has his small portfolio with the addition of a few more properties from our company. Most importantly, he has progressed as a real estate investor. He found his niche in Memphis and soon began buying properties remotely, selling them back to larger investors like our company for a small, quick profit. Sam even started a short-term lending company that lends to smaller real estate investors. He got a little off track along the way, but his early mistakes taught him the value of treating his passive investments as more than just pieces of paper that would magically perform.

Sam learned to calculate the value of his investments on more than just the price he paid or the return he thought he would receive. He learned to calculate the value based on how much time, effort, and energy he had to spend. He learned just how valuable great communication and customer service were to his overall satisfaction with his portfolio.

He also learned that he liked being an active investor and really wanted to leave the heavy lifting on his passive investments to better turnkey companies with the systems and processes in place to make his investments perform. Last, he learned that saving a few dollars by buying cheaper investments never works out the way you think it will. Cheaper does not equate to higher returns on the bottom line!

STEADY AND SYSTEMATIC

When I talk about making your investment, I'm not just talking about signing your name on the dotted line.

In the last chapter, you worked with your turnkey partner to make a plan for your investments. Now it's time to execute that plan. The right way to do this is steadily and systematically.

The first thing to remember during this process is that you are in control. The numbers are really important, and you need to understand what they are. Even though you trust your team members and allow them to advise you on decisions, you need to know the specifics of exactly what you're getting yourself into.

If you just jump into an investment with both feet, you'll find yourself blindsided: the homes are not what you thought they'd be, expenses come up that you didn't think about, the attorneys your company works with are atrocious—the list goes on and on.

There are so many moving parts in this puzzle, and to become aware of them as an investor, you really just have to experience them. Again, the best way to experience them is steadily and systematically. If you handle the investing process this way, you will always feel like you're in control, even when unexpected things come up. You will keep moving forward in the direction of your vision with as few headaches to deal with as possible.

This step of the Turnkey Safely System will walk you through the process of making your investment and show you why pacing yourself is in your best interest.

MAKE YOUR INVESTMENT

The best thing you can do when making an investment is to create a spreadsheet of the numbers, and then analyze the data.

Some key data points to keep in mind are your hard costs and soft costs. Hard costs are defined as costs that are going to occur on a set and defined basis. Taxes, insurance, principal and interest payments, property management fees, and homeowners' association fees are all examples of hard costs. Examples of soft costs include maintenance allocation, vacancy allocation, and capital expenditures (large-ticket items such as roof replacement and a water heater). These are costs that occur on an infrequent basis, but you still need to account for them, as they will definitely occur over the life of your investment.

After you make your plan with your turnkey company, the company should be able to recommend a few properties that fit your needs. This is your chance to get the details you need for your spreadsheet.

What numbers are you looking for?

To begin with, you need the price you're going to pay for the investment, as well as the appraisal of the property's value. You need the amount that the property rents for each month and the average vacancy rate or length of stay. If there's a 60-day vacancy every two years, factor that into the equation. If your company keeps the first month's rent on each new lease, take that into consideration as well.

This is where asking the right questions at the beginning really comes in handy. If you know that a company has an average length of occupancy of over four years for each property, then there is no need to account for a new lease fee each year. If you run your numbers expecting to lose a month's rent each year to a lease fee, then your numbers are never going to work and you are never going to get started.

Taxes, insurance, financing, and your company's maintenance or management costs also need to be included. You already asked your turnkey partner what percentage of collected rent its owners pay for maintenance each year, and whether it includes the maintenance markup. So, now you know exactly how much to plug into your calculations.

Now, prepare a spreadsheet—or take a sheet of paper if you're not a big fan of spreadsheets—and prepare your basic calculations.

Here are how your calculations should look:

Property Address

Price: $_____

Down Payment: $_____

Rent: $_____

Annual Net Income (Rent × 12): $_____

Hard Costs (Annual)

Taxes: $_____

Insurance: $_____

Mortgage Payments: $_____

HOA (If needed): $_____

Annual Hard Costs: $_____

Soft Costs (Annual)

Maintenance: $_____

Vacancy: $_____

Capital Improvements: $_____

Lease Fee: $_____

*If you expect to lease a property once every three years, then this should be 33% of the lease fee.

Annual Soft Costs: $_____

TOTAL Costs: $_____

Annual Gross Income: $_____
(Annual Net Income − TOTAL Costs)

Basic Net On Investment is calculated by dividing the Annual Gross Income by the Down Payment. This is calculated as a percentage.

NOI on your investment: _____%

Once you've plugged all of this data into your spreadsheet, you analyze the numbers to calculate your return on investment. What percentage return can you expect to get on your property after your costs have been factored in? Does the return meet your personal criteria? Does the annual gross income move you closer to what you need to make passively per month in order to reach your vision?

As long as the investment meets those requirements, you move forward with it. Emotional factors such as whether the house faces north or backs up to a shopping center do not play a part in this. The decision is 100 percent practical and based on facts—*not* emotions.

When it comes to turnkey real estate, you have to rely on the expert, your turnkey partner, to help guide you to make good investments. You have chosen a good company, now you have to rely on its expertise. If its logic seems faulty, such as trying to sell a two-bedroom home in a three-bedroom neighborhood or a home with no parking in a neighborhood where every home has a two-car garage, always bring your concerns to team members' attention.

I have seen many investors miss out on high-quality properties because of a "feeling" they have about a property. They don't like the interior paint colors. They prefer having flowers around the mailbox. They don't like the proximity to a mobile home park or a highway. This is where you really have to decide as an investor if you are wanting a passive or active investment.

There may be multiple times in your journey when you have to ask this question. There is nothing wrong with that. The time to make sure you want to be passive and are comfortable trusting your turnkey partner is right now—not after you have purchased a property. Your number one concern as a passive investor is not the color of the paint. Your number one concern is this: "Can my turnkey partner make this property perform the way I expect it to perform?"

These are the questions you should be answering for yourself:

- Am I comfortable that the company knows how to pick good properties?

- Does it perform high-quality renovations and eliminate deferred maintenance?

- Does it have systems and processes in place to manage my portfolio so it performs at its best?

If you can answer yes to those questions, then you can proceed.

After you give the okay to start the contract, there are a few things you should expect, and a few pitfalls you need to watch out for.

WHAT TO EXPECT

You should expect to put down earnest money. Earnest money is almost always a part of the equation, including if you are paying all cash for the property. There should be a waiting period between the time you sign a contract to purchase a property and the time you close. That is the purpose of the earnest money—to keep the property under contract while you do your proper due diligence.

When you are getting to know your turnkey team members, they should encourage you to handle the few due diligence items you need to handle, but they should also handle a smooth contract closing. That includes communicating with your lender, the title company or closing attorney, and the property inspector and property appraiser.

You should expect to be able to choose your services such as insurance, closing attorney, and inspector. Your lender will choose an appraiser to value the property. Remember, in many cases you are buying property sight unseen and far from home. You need to exercise that "letting go" muscle and trust the professionals to do their jobs. Your turnkey partner should provide you with a list of inspectors to choose from and feel free to solicit other companies yourself. This is the person that is going to be looking out for your best interest and confirming the level of renovation done to the property.

This is important. Let the inspector do her job and pay attention to the report you receive back. If there are any issues with the inspection report, listen to the response. Again, you must always pay attention to your new turnkey partner to see if there are any red flags or trouble signs. If the partner refuses to fix issues that come up on an inspection report, and we mean major issues, that is an indication that maybe it is not as good a company as you had thought. If there are minor issues like small cracks in caulk at the sink that have no bearing on the value or structural stability of the house, I wouldn't let those bother me.

You should also expect a very good, reliable attorney to handle the closing transaction, and you should be able to hire your own attorney if that's what you want to do. If for any reason your company doesn't allow you to do these things and it makes you uncomfortable, that may be a red flag—and a deal breaker.

A good company is going to have close working relationships with services that you are going to need to have a smooth closing. You may still choose to hire your own companies outside of any that your turnkey partner recommends. It should not have a problem with you doing that, but remember, it is your partner for a reason. A little earned faith goes a long way. As long as the company is earning that faith, give it some latitude, and let it help make your closing a smooth one.

PITFALLS TO AVOID

As far as pitfalls, you should *not* be expected to close on a property before the renovation is complete. You as an investor should want to see the finished product before you close. If you are not going to travel to see the house in person, and for many investors, seeing the house in person is not necessary, then you should expect to receive a Scope of Work on the property.

This will be a detailed list including pictures inside and outside, room by room, listing all the work completed on the property. It should include pictures of a new roof, new AC unit, new water heater and other systems, new tile, fixtures, flooring, paint, and detailed exterior work. If your turnkey partner spent time working on a property, it needs to be able to document that work for you.

You should also be prepared for costs to change. The insurance may come in slightly more than you thought it was, or the house may appraise slightly low. When these things happen, don't immediately jump to the conclusion that you're being hoodwinked. You should have such a high level of comfort with your turnkey partner at this point that changes like these should be easy conversations. And if you're not comfortable with the solutions to the changes, then don't close on the property.

Things will happen when you close on a property. A good turnkey partner will help you solve the problems that come up.

This is why I advised you early on to be patient and spend your time getting to know the partner or partners you choose. Some investors will look at little challenges that come up as major problems. If you take your time and get to know the turnkey partner you are choosing to work with, then these conversations are easy. Even if you are not satisfied and choose to go in a different direction, the conversation is easy. Address any issues steadily and systematically, and keep moving forward. Either the property is a right fit for your portfolio or it is not.

PACE YOURSELF

Investing steadily and systematically is a process you go through with each investment. But more than that, it's a principle that applies to the execution of your larger plan as well.

Your plan can and should involve purchasing multiple properties. A complete portfolio includes a minimum of four houses, and eventually you need a portfolio to minimize your risk and keep your investments growing steadily. However, that doesn't mean you need to buy them all at once. Most of the time, it's in your best interest to build your portfolio two or three houses at a time. If you need four houses, then you buy two or three up front, and if all goes well, you complete your portfolio within a year or two.

Give your turnkey partner a chance to earn your additional business by hitting your expectations. Make it earn your trust, and then reward yourself by building out your portfolio.

You do this to make the company you're doing business with earn its reputation with you. If you've done your due diligence, you have a high level of comfort with the company before you start, and that's fine. But buying your investments at a planned pace rather than all at once is an extra safety mechanism for you as the investor. If you purchase a property and it turns out that your company isn't as great as you thought it was, you're going to be glad you have only two or three houses with it and not five.

TURNKEY MASTERY TIPS

Harness the power of multiple properties

I always recommend that investors build a portfolio and take advantage of the power of scaling to multiple properties all providing income at the same time. There are two major reasons why I don't recommend buying just one property to begin with. The first is that you're able to take advantage of scale and negotiate better pricing on some of the services if you close more than one property at a time. The second reason is that having multiple properties lowers risk.

As an investor, you will be on a roller coaster. When your property is occupied and paying you a return, you are 100 percent occupied and happy. When your property is vacant or behind in the rent, you are 100 percent vacant and unhappy. Who needs the aggravation of everything hanging on a single property? If your vision requires you to set a goal of just one property, don't buy turnkey. Figure out another vision with a bigger goal!

On the other hand, don't let your turnkey partner pressure you into buying too many properties at once. Less reputable partners may say something like, "You really have to buy these houses now, because these great deals are going to be gone later." A quality turnkey company will never say something like that to you. The truth is that there is no perfect time to invest. You simply have to get started. You should absolutely start by building a portfolio, but don't get fooled into thinking you have to buy the first five properties you are shown before all the good deals are gone. You can find good turnkey investments that pay you consistent returns in almost any market around the country at any given time. Anyone who tells you otherwise is using a scare tactic.

Most investors don't need to buy all their properties at once in order to reach their goals. Turnkey is a long-term investment, and that means you have time to execute your larger plan. So exercise patience.

Pick up properties at a pace you're comfortable with. Figure out how the system works. Get comfortable with the processes your turnkey partner uses, and make it earn your trust. Remember, *you* are in control. Instead of risking everything before you've gathered some experience, give yourself time.

The more you invest, the more you learn. And the better you pace yourself with your investments, the better those investments will become over time.

SAFETY IN NUMBERS

A steady and systematic mindset is your safest bet as a turnkey real estate investor. Remember that this is a long-term investment. It's about the numbers and the fundamentals, and about how your turnkey partner shows you that it can make those fundamentals perform over time. Never lose sight of the long game. Don't invest in properties based on what they're doing right now. Look at how they're going to help you 20 years from now. Be honest with yourself about your vision, and *always* keep your eye on your long-term plan.

When you make your investment with these cornerstones in mind, you will set yourself up for the success you're looking for as a member of the turnkey revolution.

But you're not done yet. Investing in passive real estate doesn't mean being passive. In the next chapter, I'll show you how to follow up with your investments so you can manage the most profitable portfolio possible with an eye to the long term.

THE TURNKEY SAFELY CHECKLIST

Making Your Investment

- Do I have all the numbers I need to calculate my return?

- Does the calculated return on my potential investment meet my personal criteria?

- Am I able to choose an insurance company and attorney that make me feel comfortable?

- Am I moving forward with my investments at a steady pace?

TURNKEY MASTERY TIPS

Turnkey is a great launching pad for future investments.

There are literally thousands of different ways to make money in real estate. Most require a lot of active participation on the part of the investor, but there are also ways to build an active business around passive real estate investing. If you are passionate about real estate and looking for a place to start, turnkey real estate is a great jumping-off point. It allows you to learn many of the ins and outs of real estate while safely building a portfolio. I have worked with many real estate investors who have used their turnkey experience as a launching pad for other real estate investments.

In the end, it's about what's right for you.

Don't make investments just because they look good on paper or based on slick marketing material. Make investments because they fit *your* plan.

FOLLOW UP WITH YOUR INVESTMENTS

Two brothers-in-law, Steve and David, invested with our company. Steve was a highly engaged investor who was in contact with us monthly. David, not so much. Steve was also excellent at managing his manager—meaning that he always examined his monthly statements, and if we made an error he was going to catch it. I liked that about him. It showed that while he may be an active investor, his turnkey portfolio was the key to his vision and he stayed on top of it.

I was personally in contact with Steve every few months as he and I had become friends. One day, during a conversation, Steve mentioned to me that David wasn't happy with his investments.

"David just got a $250 maintenance bill," Steve said. "He's really upset. He says he doesn't think turnkey is a good investment for him, and he's thinking of selling everything."

I promised Steve that I would look into it and find out what was going on.

And I did. When I pulled David's records up, I found that he owned 14 properties with us—and he knew almost nothing about them. He never took our monthly phone calls. He was very poor at responding to emails. He hardly ever spoke with us throughout the year at all. I assumed after looking at his track record of communication that he was probably not looking at his monthly statements either. It was a safe assumption.

David was making an impressive 15.5 percent return on his money every year. You don't find investments like those very often. Anyone would jump at the chance to take assets performing that well off his hands. The $250 bill he had gotten was a drop in the bucket when it came to the big scope of his portfolio.

But David had no idea how well he was doing because he never followed up. He had put himself in a position where he was ready to drop thousands of dollars in profit over a $250 footnote.

And that's only the beginning of why staying engaged with your turnkey portfolio is critical to your long-term success as an investor.

PREPARE TO ENGAGE

The term *passive investing* often gives people an incorrect idea of what turnkey real estate involves. *Passive* in this case applies to the way you acquire and build a portfolio. It doesn't describe the process you use to manage that portfolio once you own it.

In fact, the opposite is true: once you have your portfolio, you need to be consistently proactive in following up with it. This is a key step in the Turnkey Safely System. You always have to check the returns and economics of your investments. Paperwork, insurance, tax statements—these are just a few of the things you have to stay on top of as a turnkey investor over the long term.

Why? Even the best companies out there are subject to human error. That's why you should take nothing on faith. You can't afford to assume that you weren't double charged for a management fee or a maintenance item. You can't assume that you received everything you're supposed to receive each month. You can't assume that you have the best insurance rate or that your property taxes shouldn't have been lowered. These are small items, but they add up to a very big picture. You, as the investor, have to take a look at each little way you can squeeze out a little more return. Just a once-a-year checkup can make a world of difference.

Not only should you keep an eye on where you can save, you have to check your statements and take the calls from your turnkey partner, even if you think everything is going well. When you take the time to follow up on a regular basis, you'll find that your comfort level is much higher and the stress level of owning a $100,000 property from a thousand miles away is erased. Not only will you sleep better at night, but you'll empower yourself to make good decisions about the long-term goals of your personal turnkey revolution.

You won't want to throw out investments that are giving you 15 percent returns, even if you do get a $250 maintenance bill now and then.

In this chapter, I'll take you through the checklist of how to follow up with your turnkey investments and show you why communication with your company can be a make-or-break factor in your long-term success.

THE FOLLOW-UP CHECKLIST

Your turnkey follow-up checklist is a process that works on three levels: things you need to follow up with on a monthly basis, a yearly basis, and an ongoing basis over time.

Monthly follow-up

On a monthly basis, you need to review the rental ledger that your management company sends you.

Your ledger should include rent collected for the current month, rent collected for previous months, management fees, and maintenance issues. When you look at the ledger, you're checking for any missing rents, duplicate charges, or overcharges. As I stated before, this is a people business, and human error is involved almost daily. There are a lot of moving parts, and small $50 charges add up over time. You have to pay attention to the invoices, maintenance bills, and management charges. This takes a few minutes each month.

Your turnkey partner should also call you once a month to update you on your investment. You need to make sure you take that call so that your company can update you on anything unusual that's going on with your property. This is also your opportunity to ask questions about your portfolio. Having this live communication with your turnkey partner is one of the most critical parts of managing your investments successfully. I'll explain this in greater depth later in this chapter.

Yearly follow-up

You also need to review certain aspects of your investments on an annual basis.

I explained why this review normally includes seeing if you can reduce your insurance costs and taxes. It's important that you don't forget taxes and insurance. These are some of the only fixed costs you have when you invest in turnkey, so it can be easy not to think about them, but they do matter. Even if you have to change insurance carriers to get a lower rate, it's worth it, because anything you save on insurance and taxes flows straight to your bottom line.

Your turnkey partner can usually help you with both insurance and taxes. An established company has leverage in these areas because of its size and track record. For instance, Memphis Invest was managing more than 3,000 properties in 2015. Our houses are managed well, with few vacancies and very low vandalism rates—things that are music to an insurance company's ears.

We approached a national insurance provider and worked with it to create an insurance product based on our portfolio. That insurance program helped drive down insurance costs for owners by over 20 percent. Now, not everyone uses our insurance, but there is an option, and if it saves an investor money and increases his return, then our size and record helped us to improve the investor's experience. That is what you are looking for: a company that can use its leverage to improve your experience as a real estate investor.

Your company's scale can help you in the tax area as well. Again, to take Memphis Invest as an example, if half of our 3,000 owners wanted to challenge the values of their properties to lower their property taxes, our company would be able to negotiate a low fee for a local attorney to handle that for them. In almost all of those scenarios, the attorney charges only if she is able to reduce the tax percentage, so our clients don't even need to pay that fee if the challenge isn't successful.

Don't get complacent about what seem like small charges such as insurance and taxes, because they can save you thousands of dollars in the long run. Too often, real estate investors pay close attention to rental amounts and interest rates, which are very important. But, the often-overlooked expenses need to be checked on a regular basis as well. Every year, look for ways to save on your fixed investment costs, and take action if you have to.

Ongoing follow-up

In addition to your monthly and yearly reviews, you also need to manage certain things about your investments that change over time. Specifically, you want to be aware of tier pricing options with your turnkey company.

Tier pricing is common to most management companies. The company will charge you certain rates for specific services when you have one or two houses with it, but offer you discounts on those same services as you add to your portfolio. For example, the management fee for one house may be 10 percent, but it may drop to 9 percent when you own five houses, or 8 percent when you own ten. Or the company may waive its standard convenience fee with a resident to extend his lease. These fees are often waived or lowered for an investor with a larger portfolio.

Find out what your turnkey partner's benchmarks are for tier pricing, and keep tabs on them. If your partner doesn't have a set program, then volume purchasing and management may be items you can negotiate. Most major companies are going to offer tier pricing discounts. Do you hit the next tier and start getting discounts when you hit five houses? Seven houses? Ten houses? Once you reach those milestones, it reduces the cost of your whole portfolio. Just like staying on top of your taxes and insurance, anything you save here will flow straight to your bottom line.

You never want to throw your plan out the window just to hit tier pricing benchmarks. However, if you've been following up and you see that you're not stretching yourself too much, it's okay to push to get to the next milestone a little earlier to drive down your overall cost.

KEEP IN TOUCH

You went through a lot to find and choose a good turnkey partner for your investments. The follow-up stage of the process is where you hold that partner accountable for all the things it agreed to do for you when you signed on with the company.

I explained in Chapter 6 why choosing a good partner is a make-or-break factor in your success as a turnkey investor. You may be investing in a property hundreds or thousands of miles away from you, over which you do not have direct physical control. You cannot afford to accept bad management, *period.* Staying in touch with your company on a regular basis is how you verify that you're getting the service you need and deserve.

Your turnkey company should make it easy for you to stay in touch. It should have an online portal where you can print your statements and see what's going on with your account in real time regarding rents collected, bills, and notices sent to residents. Remember the phone call I told you to ask about receiving? Not only should you receive a phone call every single month, but that phone call should be from the same person each time so that you can build a relationship with someone who understands your specific needs.

Almost every time we have an issue with a client, it's just the result of poor communication. And on the flip side of that coin, the vast majority of our clients who are happy with their investments have terrific relationships with their customer service contacts in our company.

HOW A WIN TURNS INTO A LOSS

Every company should have a person who takes the tough calls from upset clients. For my company, that person is an owner—me. I jump on the phone with any upset client to listen and try to figure out how we can help. In almost every scenario, the real issue at heart is a lack of communication.

Communication is key. You cannot be passive about your passive investments.

In one conversation, I had an investor out of Los Angeles furious with me over the poor performance of his single investment property. He had never pushed forward with his plan to build a portfolio and never purchased any additional properties. Now he found himself on the up and down roller coaster. In fact, his investment was only going up, but he couldn't see the big picture. The real problem was that he had only talked to his customer service rep once in four years. Now he was having his very first vacancy in four years, and it was a good-sized bill. His first response was that he was getting ripped off and he wanted out. He demanded that we help him sell his property immediately. I reviewed the performance of his one property and explained to him that in four years, after factoring in his maintenance costs with the move-out, he had earned an astonishing 68 percent return on his investment. But he was so worked up and so convinced that he had made a bad investment, that he didn't care what I said.

So I offered to buy his property back on the spot. I reasoned that with these types of returns, there would be investors lined up to add this property to their portfolio. We purchased his property back, and after closing costs, he made a substantial return on his initial investment. And yet he lost.

He lost the opportunity to build his portfolio and use turnkey real estate to fulfill his long-term vision. Even though to his way of thinking he was winning in the short term, in the end he lost.

When you consistently engage with your turnkey partner team members, they will fight for you. At Memphis Invest, our customer service team members come to us on a daily basis and say, "I just got off the phone with this client, and an issue came up with his property. I've been speaking to him every month for the last year, and I'd like to help him out." The rep asks if she can waive a maintenance fee, or if the company can cover an unexpected cost.

It goes beyond management. Things happen in our clients' lives every day: babies are born, people get married, people pass away. When those events occur, our reps come to us and say, "I'd like to send flowers," or "This person just had a baby. Can we send her a onesie that says 'future investor'?" These little things bring great joy to us as a company, and they happen only because of the bond we build with our investors.

So, for your own satisfaction, always pick up the phone when your turnkey company rep calls you each month. Talk to your partner. See how things are going. Your level of trust and comfort with your company will rise every time you do.

As long as you follow this process, from setting a strong vision before you start to keeping in touch with your company after the investments have been made, you will set yourself up for the best possible experience investing in turnkey real estate. And once you have this system in place, it can expand as your vision does. I'll explain the limitless potential of the turnkey revolution in the next chapter.

THE TURNKEY SAFELY CHECKLIST

Following up with Your Investments

- Do I consistently check my monthly ledger for missing rents, duplicate charges, and overcharges?

- Do I reevaluate my investments for taxes and insurance savings each year?

- Am I keeping track of the tier pricing levels offered by my turnkey company?

- Do I talk to my turnkey partner by phone every month?

- Is the person I touch base with at my company the same individual each month?

TURNKEY MASTERY TIPS

You cannot be passive about your passive investments.

There may not be a more important tip in this book. Buying a turnkey property and building your portfolio passively does not mean that you completely abdicate your role to some company in a remote city. It does the heavy lifting, but you still have to keep track of your portfolio's performance. As noted in the Turnkey Safely Checklist questions above, the best way to avoid mistakes is by checking your statements each month and consistently talking with your management company. These are the habits of a successful turnkey investor.

EXPAND YOUR VISION

Charlene was a single, older woman from the Northeast who had spent years of time and thousands of dollars on real estate education. She knew that real estate was the path for her, and she truly wanted to be an investor. But she was having a tough time getting her foot in the door.

In a field where most people are loud and decisive, Charlene was on the shy side.

She wasn't a take-charge kind of person, and she didn't stand out in any way at all. On top of that, she was meek and soft-spoken. She was as invisible as you can get—and she had zero confidence in herself.

Charlene tried asking people for advice, but nobody was all that interested in helping her. She tried wholesaling properties at her local Real Estate Investment Association (REIA) with no luck. No one listened to her, both because she was timid and, more important, because she wasn't even an investor yet.

Then, finally, someone told Charlene about our turnkey company. She came to Memphis for an open house weekend of ours, and she decided to give us a try. That same weekend, she bought five houses with us. After years of struggling, Charlene was finally an investor. She felt good about her decision. For the first time, she felt confident that she could really do this.

One year later, Charlene told us a story.

"A few weeks after I invested with you, I went back to my usual REIA group with another wholesale property," she said. "And this time, I got up on stage, with a microphone and everything. I told everybody in that room, 'I'm a real estate investor who owns five properties, and I have a wholesale deal. Who wants to talk to me about it?' Right after I got off stage, multiple people came up to me. They wanted to do business."

Charlene had moved from studying real estate to taking action and investing in it. And that had opened up the pathway for her to move in the direction she wanted to go.

JUST THE BEGINNING

Many people talk about investing in real estate. Few take action. Real estate makes for great dinner party conversation. There is a world of difference between talk and action, though. The few who actually take action are special. They are the ones who are taking their futures and their visions into their own hands.

By the time you complete the process outlined in this book, you belong to the latter group. And once you become an active member of the turnkey revolution, your goals and vision will actually start to become real in your life. Everything will move forward. You will begin to reach the milestones and arrive at the places you wanted to go.

That's a terrific feeling. But when it happens, a new question comes up: "What's next for me?"

What's next is to expand your vision—the final step in the Turnkey Safely System. No matter how far you go, you can always find a way to broaden your horizons, both in terms of personal goals and as an investor. This chapter will give you a preview of what you can expect as you continue on the road to real estate.

GO WHERE THE GROWTH IS

Life never goes stagnant.

Your life and your investments both improve as time goes on. As they do, your vision expands and blossoms right along with them. One day, you suddenly find yourself with more disposable income than you thought you were going to have. Or maybe when you first made your plan five years ago, it was perfect for you because you were single, but now you're married and you have a child, and the plan you had doesn't support your new life.

You took the necessary risks to achieve your dreams, and you succeeded. But now you have a new vision and a new idea of your perfect day. And you need a new plan to go along with them.

As you grow as an investor, you will see opportunities that weren't there before. So much more becomes available to you once you reach your original goal. Maybe you want to expand your portfolio to include multifamily homes. Maybe you feel ready to branch out to other turnkey markets with multiple companies, or to multiple markets using the same company. Maybe you want to try your hand at different types of real estate investing.

Whatever the case, taking action and being consistent with your first plan will lead you to the next one. Not only will you see the way forward, but you'll also have greater confidence to keep walking down that road.

The more you grow, the more you'll be able to keep growing. Your turnkey investments have the ability to grow with you, and you can use them to support any goal you can imagine. Just keep expanding your vision, and go where the growth is.

THE FIRST STEP

Everything starts with taking that one first step.

If turnkey real estate sounds like a good fit for you, but you don't know what to do or who to talk to first, Memphis Invest offers additional resources to help you make a plan for moving forward, available at www.MemphisInvest.com/QuickStart.

You can access these resources risk free, without worrying about being sold on properties that aren't right for you. Our company is very proud of the fact that we say no to many more potential investors than we say yes to, because we want you to have the perfect experience investing, whether that's with us or someone else. We want to make sure that your needs are actually a good fit for what we have to offer.

And when I say that, I mean it.

Back in 2013, I met with a broker out of New York City, a tall gentleman by the name of Byron. "I love your company," he told me animatedly. "I cannot wait to get started with you guys." Then he launched into an explanation of all the real estate investing he'd done so far: the flips he was doing, the properties he already owned, everything he did when he went to go see them to buy and manage them well.

I remember how excited he was to tell me the details of his latest multifamily property in New Jersey. How he had picked the colors for the inside and refinished the original hardwood floors. He had prospective residents lining up before he had the property finished. He told me of his weekend routine and how it included driving by his properties to make sure they were the best in the neighborhood.

I knew from our conversation that I was talking to some-one who truly loved real estate. He had a vision, too. He had a concrete vision for how real estate was going to lead him away from his full-time job and give him his time back. He knew exactly how many properties he wanted to own, and when he explained how he wanted to spend his time, it was clear he had put a lot of time and thought into how to achieve his vision.

This was one of those conversations that I wished could have gone on all morning. I was really enjoying myself, but I knew the hard part was coming.

"I've got money, and I'm ready to go," he said, full of excite-ment. "Where do we start?"

I looked him in the eye and said, "We don't."

His eyebrows went up. "Why?" he asked.

"Because from everything you just told me, you're a hands-on real estate investor—and you love it," I explained. "You're finding, buying, selling, generating activity, making money here in New York and New Jersey. I've got suburban homes, and not only is there very little activity on the houses them-selves, there's zero activity for you. How are you going to feel about sending me half a million dollars to own five houses that you won't have a say in the management of, at all? Passive investing isn't what drives you. It's not what makes you happy."

When we were done that morning, Byron reached over and shook my hand. "You know, that's probably what makes you guys so great," he said. "You're willing to tell somebody no who was going to buy houses, because you know I won't be happy."

The truth of the matter was, if I tried to make everyone happy who said they wanted to buy houses from me, I'd be deal-ing with a bunch of investors like Jack from earlier and making no one happy. There was no way I could provide great customer service to Byron and provide great service to my other clients. I would spend too much time and energy on Byron. I knew that we were not the right investment, and by saying no, I could meet the needs of our other clients—the ones whose needs match perfectly with what we provide.

The way you treat people matters. We truly believe that you can have anything you want in life, if you honestly help other people get what they want. And everything we've done has been built around that conviction.

PEOPLE FIRST

The personal relationships we have with our clients are why we go to work each day.

The impact of what we do constantly amazes us. We've helped people transform not just their own lives with turn-key investing, but the lives of their families as well. Our clients have taken their parents' retirement funds out of buildings that weren't doing anything and invested that money in single-family homes with us instead. They've used vehicles like 1031 exchange programs to sell large properties tax free and reinvest those funds into turnkey portfolios. Their parents now have a comfortable monthly income that will support them through their golden years.

We've also had clients who have had to put their lives on hold when their children were affected by life-changing illnesses. When scenarios like that happen, suddenly nothing matters to us but how that person's portfolio performs. The team pulls together and sends gifts to the hospital. Anything that happens with that client's properties—vacancies, repair fees—we just handle quietly at no cost to him or her in the hope of making the person's life a little bit easier.

When you have the ability to affect somebody's life like that, it changes your whole outlook on why you do what you do. There's a lot to be said for personal relationships. Wherever you invest in turnkey, take the time to build that relationship with your team, and everyone will benefit.

ACT ON SUCCESS

At the end of the day, turnkey real estate investing comes down to this: you need to be bold enough to take action if you want to find success.

Action doesn't mean jumping into your investments with blinders on. It means moving forward patiently and methodically. It means understanding the calculated risks you're taking, and making decisions based on facts over emotions.

It takes courage and confidence to walk the path to success. And you will find both the courage and the confidence you need by moving forward steadily and systematically, staying focused on your vision.

Remember, you became a "real" real estate investor from the moment you took those first steps planning a portfolio of homes to build your vision. Now as you continue to move systematically toward your goals, celebrate your small successes along the way, and continue to build upon them, evolving and fine-tuning your vision.

Nothing makes me happier than hearing back from investors who have continued to build their portfolios and moved beyond those first few homes that they started with. Stories like Charlene's and Sam's, who both became active real estate investors after starting with turnkey properties. Those are the most satisfying conversations for me.

Now, it's your turn!

THE TURNKEY SAFELY CHECKLIST

Expanding Your Vision

🔑 What actions am I taking to continue building my portfolio and move closer to my vision?

🔑 Am I continuing to be inspired by my turnkey company to review my portfolio, my goals, and my vision?

🔑 Where is my confidence today as a turnkey real estate investor? What concrete steps can I take to feel even stronger about my investments?

TURNKEY MASTERY TIP

A great partner understands your goals for the long term.

Turnkey is a people business. Your turnkey partner should be a partner in your success. If it is not willing to forgo a few dollars on a deal here or there to make sure you succeed, then keep looking. This is your partner for the lifetime of your portfolio. For some that is going to be a very long time. A great partner is one that understands that your dreams, plans, goals, and vision are all very real things, and is willing to work hand in hand with you to make them come true.

NOW IT'S YOUR TURN

I found myself on stage in Denver, Colorado, on a morning in February 2017. I was speaking at the Best Real Estate Investing Advice Ever Conference sponsored by Joe Fairless. His podcast has thousands of listeners, and he had gathered a few hundred investors to listen to speakers like myself share our advice. I had spent two days listening to speakers and panels giving their best advice, and I knew I was about to shake up the conversation.

I had come into the conference with an article in mind warning of the dangers in turnkey real estate. I decided to test the subject on my listeners. I started my talk off with a few light thank-yous and some remarks about what we had heard so far. I always have a few funny one-liners to engage with the crowd. Then I unleashed one line that quieted the room.

"A lot of investors are going to lose money buying turnkey real estate today."

If I was trying to get everyone's attention, it worked. The room grew quiet. There were a lot of puzzled looks. After all, I was the guy in the room that was supposed to explain how turnkey real estate worked. I was there to answer questions and clear up any misconceptions about what was the true definition of turnkey real estate—and that was exactly what I intended to do.

This was a conference with a lot of short talks, so I didn't have any time to waste.

"Investors are going to lose money buying turnkey real estate today because they are buying the word *turnkey* without any thought of what that really means," I explained. "In most cases the word is nothing more than a marketing term used to attract your interest. If you want to buy turnkey real estate safely, you have to follow a very specific outline of steps."

I spent the next 30 minutes explaining what would become the Turnkey Safely System and how passive investors could follow its steps to safely buy property anywhere in the world from the comfort of their home. And I showed investors how to avoid companies using the word *turnkey* to market their properties when they didn't own the properties, and when they didn't do any work on the properties, or even offer qualified in-house management.

The audience was furiously taking notes, so I kept going.

I broke down the dangers of buying cheap properties for $50,000 that had thousands of dollars in deferred maintenance. I explained the dangers of buying properties from a turnkey company that had popped up just 12 months earlier after the owner had bought a few properties and suddenly wanted to "teach" other investors how to buy turnkey properties from him.

When I opened the floor to questions from the audience, I was hit with comment after comment about how unexpected it was to hear from someone in the turnkey industry advising *against* just jumping in with both feet. The audience was truly surprised that for once someone had told them that being passive about their passive investments would lose them money. They were really shocked to hear that in some cases, being told no was the greatest gift they could be given by someone in the real estate world.

Hopefully you can tell from this book how passionate I am about helping investors buy turnkey real estate safely. I didn't have the help I needed when I first started investing, and I paid a steep price for it. As a result of my experience, I've made it my mission to be honest and up front with investors about the right and wrong ways to build your portfolio. I had a vision for my future, and I almost lost it all by making really bad investment decisions. This book is my attempt to help others avoid my mistakes so they can marry their vision with a safe, long-term turnkey investment strategy.

Anyone can buy turnkey real estate. All it takes is the knowledge to do it safely and the confidence to have high expectations and not settle for mediocre properties, renovations, and service.

When I finished my talk that morning, I concluded with a reminder to everyone in the audience. I explained that while some investors will lose money buying turnkey real estate, none of the folks in attendance needed to be on that list. No one reading this book has to either. There is a specific formula you can follow to protect your turnkey investments. A formula to help you raise your expectations and ask the right questions. You can put any turnkey company to the Turnkey Test and rest assured that if it passes, you can safely start building your portfolio.

This book is your own personal study guide. Learn from the lessons and stories I've shared. Follow the steps I've laid out, and get started building your own personal turnkey portfolio.

TIME FOR ACTION

You will never hear me tell investors that they need to get started building their portfolio today before they miss all the good deals. I simply don't believe that to be true. However, there is no better time than today to get crystal clear on what your vision is for your future. There is no better time than today to start building your plan to get there.

Looking back at the 1,800 plus real estate investors we have worked with over the years, I know the power of small actions. The first steps you take as an investor to get started are the ones that will forever change your life.

You have always had the opportunity to invest in real estate, anywhere in the world. Now you have what you need to do it safely and passively.

Be brave, take action, and go do exactly what you've always wanted to do.

Become a real estate investor in the turnkey revolution.

Bring your future to life, one turnkey property at a time.

THE TURNKEY SAFELY CHECKLIST

I first wrote the Turnkey Safely Checklist when I was building my own portfolio for the second time. I had already made enough mistakes to last me a lifetime and promised myself I wouldn't ever make the same mistakes twice.

So, I made a list to guide my next decisions, and even to this day, every time I add a property to my portfolio, I follow this list. I have invested in four different states and seven different cities and have plans to add more. Each time I consider adding to my portfolio, I go through the same checklist and honestly assess the ways in which I am achieving my goals and building my vision. I always ask myself if a particular investment property or investment decision moves me closer to my goals and vision, and I evolve my plans over time.

With this checklist to guide me, I no longer accept "feeling" good about buying a property. I have a high level of confidence every time I decide to add a new turnkey property to my passive portfolio. Following a set of processes protects me and keeps me moving forward.

Here are my answers to the Turnkey Safely Checklist. I hope my answers will help guide you to making great decisions building your turnkey portfolio!

Getting Started

🔑 What is my background in real estate?

At this point, I am totally comfortable buying real estate. I have purchased 5 homes for me and my family to live in and close to 75 for my personal portfolio.

🔑 Have I bought my first home to live in?

Yes.

🔑 Have I bought my first investment property?

Yes.

🔑 Do I have friends or family who have invested in real estate?

Yes, I have both family and friends who have invested in real estate including some who have lost money.

🔑 Do I have a local real estate investors club to attend?

I have a couple of groups that I can meet with. I have only heard good things about one of them, so I'll start there.

Is Turnkey Right for Me?

🔑 Do I want to be hands-on or hands-off with my investments?

This is a tough question for me since I like to be hands-on and know about all of my investments. But I don't have the same investment opportunities nearby, and I know I need a professional manager to hold the residents accountable. So overall, I think I will be comfortable with the right management company.

🔑 Do I want a quick return, or am I in it for the long game?

I want to build a long-term portfolio that may have a generational impact for my family. I want that portfolio to be passive, so turnkey is the right way to fulfill my long-term strategy.

🔑 Do I need to be close to my investment, or can I handle the distance?

I have always wanted to be close to my investments. As I have grown in experience, however, I have realized that being near my investments has probably hurt more than it has helped me. I am completely comfortable investing far from where I live so long as I am following the steps I set up to do it safely and correctly.

🔑 Do I have enough money to get started?

Yes. I have enough money set aside for my passive portfolio to purchase two to five turnkey properties to get me started with an average price point of $100,000 to $125,000. That is with me putting 25 percent down on each property and covering closing costs.

Finding Your "Why"

🔑 What is most important to me? What two or three things would I keep if I had to give up everything else?

My family is the most important thing to me without a doubt. My five kids and my wife are my everything, and they help inspire me. Providing opportunity and seeing their joy is very important. Second, giving away money to charitable causes is almost as satisfying as making money in the first place, so I definitely want to create the environment where I have the resources I need to contribute to good causes.

What does my perfect day look like?

My perfect day is definitely spent near the water. I can smell the salt of the sea and hear the birds outside. More than anything else, my perfect day is built around me doing the things that make me happiest. It's not about being retired, but about being able to decide and do the things I want to do each day. Isn't that what retirement is, anyway? So, my perfect day is all about my family!

Setting a Path

What are the top five investing goals that will take me to my vision?

Buy two or three properties per year.

Buy in markets far from me offering lower price points and hiring professionals.

Use the cash flow from my properties to reduce principle. I don't need the income.

View each property as my kids' college fund or my retirement. Not as properties.

Only buy the assets that fit my plan. I will be disciplined and will not get knocked off of my plan.

Financial Planning

🔑 What resources do I have to get started?

I am putting a portion of my monthly income into an account for savings that I will use as a down payment and closing costs on each property. I already have savings set aside for college and retirement that we are going to use to buy assets providing income. We are going to use the cash flow to reduce the debt and own the properties faster. I have a good credit score and a spouse with a good credit score, and we both are working. I have an IRA that I can move into a SDIRA. All of these are assets we can use to build our portfolio.

🔑 How much money will I need to build my portfolio?

I estimate that it will take between $400,000 and $500,000 over the next four to six years to build my portfolio. It could take much less, but I am estimating high and planning on buying the best properties possible and not settling for cheap properties.

🔑 What are the hard costs that come with owning a turnkey investment property?

Interest Rate

Appraisal fee (one-time cost)

Inspection fee (one-time cost)

Closing costs (one-time fees)

Taxes

Insurance

Using a Self-Directed IRA to Buy Turnkey Real Estate

🔑 Do you have an IRA that you can convert or an SDIRA already set up?

Not yet, but I need to get one set up and check to see if my wife and kids can have one too.

🔑 How much is in your IRA accounts?

N/A

🔑 What are you allowed to invest in with your SDIRA?

Almost anything, as long as it is not owned by me or part of my direct family.

🔑 What is disqualified for you as an investment with your SDIRA?

I cannot invest in things with my family. I cannot invest in collectibles or insurance policies.

🔑 What are the most crucial qualities in a good SDIRA company?

Experience

Knowledge

Communication

🔑 What are two warning signs of fraud when investing your SDIRA?

Unsolicited investment offers

Guaranteed returns

Researching the Market

Have I put in a lot of time and effort to research markets of interest to me?

Yes. I want to invest in markets that give me the best opportunity for my money to be protected, whether I am familiar with the market or not.

Does this market I'm interested in have strong population stability and economic growth potential?

Yes, each of the markets I invest in and even other markets on my list that I have not invested in have strong economic outlooks. They are all different, with different strengths and weaknesses, but they are all strong and stable.

Does this market have a local business journal?

Yes.

What have I learned about this market from reading the local business journal, chamber of commerce brochure, and local blogs?

I am much more confident in the markets because I have taken the time to read what is going on behind the scenes. I've read about everything from the rosy predictions to the dirt from the alleyways.

Taking all of this under consideration, does this market pass the research funnel test?

Yes.

Choosing Your Turnkey Company

🔑 Are there any turnkey companies available in my target city?

Yes, they are XXX Invest and YYY Investments.

🔑 Does my potential turnkey company have a strong online presence?

Yes. There are a lot of different white papers, videos, and customer testimonials that help me get educated and a behind-the-scenes look.

🔑 Am I satisfied with my potential company's answers to the Turnkey Test?

Yes.

🔑 Does my potential company offer stock that meets my investing needs?

One company has properties that are a little riskier and in riskier neighborhoods, while the other is more expensive, but definitely less risky. I'm going with the higher priced, lower risk company.

🔑 Am I signing on with my company based on value instead of price?

Absolutely!

Creating an Investment Plan

🔑 Did I sit down with my team to create an investment plan, or have I been trying to do it all by myself?

One of the reasons I loved my team is that they were patient and spent time working with me. I never felt rushed. I knew there was demand for their product, but I never felt like I had to move quick to keep working with them. They made me feel comfortable and answered my questions patiently.

🔑 How many properties do I need to include in my portfolio to reach my vision?

10.

🔑 What is my time frame for purchasing these properties?

Two or three properties per year with a plan to have all ten within four years.

🔑 Does my plan take into consideration . . .

- My long-term financial goals?

Yes. I want to use my portfolio to provide funding for my kids' education, their weddings, and even our retirement. Our ultimate vision would be to give our kids a wedding present of a paid-off rental property to help them get started in life. The properties will be in nice enough neighborhoods where they could either live there or keep them for passive income.

- The steps I've taken so far toward meeting those financial goals?

Yes. I have included not only the steps I've taken in passive income, but also included my other investments.

- What kind of risk I'm comfortable with, and how much?

I want to reduce risk by buying the best properties I can in the best locations. That means they will be more expensive, but they will attract a higher qualified client. I want to buy above the median home price with above median rent rates. I think this will hold down my vacancy and maintenance.

- The level of portfolio diversification that will work best for me?

Yes. By focusing on these types of neighborhoods and properties, I will see fewer opportunities, but they will be the better opportunities. I can diversify across multiple cities and have fewer investors competing for these properties since most are attracted to lower price levels.

Making Your Investment

Do I have all the numbers I need to calculate my return?

Yes. I know what my hard costs will be, and I can reduce my vacancy and maintenance to a minimum based on the property I buy.

🔑 Does the calculated return on my potential investment meet my personal criteria?

Yes. I am okay with a lower return but higher cash flow by putting a larger down payment on each property. I will use the additional cash flow to reduce the principle and can hopefully own the property outright more quickly.

🔑 Am I able to choose an insurance company and attorney that make me feel comfortable?

Yes. This was a big deal because several companies I looked at would not let me use my own attorney. They wanted to require me to use their services. Ultimately, a company that makes suggestions and requires that I use their list made perfect sense so long as they provided good service and competitive pricing. Not having a choice was not an option for me.

🔑 Am I moving forward with my investments at a steady pace?

My plan is to buy two or three a year—and yes, I am on pace.

Following up with Your Investments

🔑 Do I consistently check my monthly ledger for missing rents, duplicate charges, and overcharges?

Yes. Every month I look at my ledger to make sure my direct deposit matches my statement.

Do I reevaluate my investments for taxes and insurance savings each year?

Yes. I have challenged increases in taxes and ask for a reduction in insurance costs each year.

Am I keeping track of the tier pricing levels offered by my turnkey company?

Yes. Essentially, the companies I have chosen have lower-cost properties that are right at median price for a market and higher price properties in nicer neighborhoods. They also have properties that they build from the ground up that are more expensive. This gives me a range to choose from when building my portfolio, but they do not offer cheap price properties. They do not offer discounts, but their services such as management and maintenance are reduced if I build a portfolio with more properties.

Do I talk to my turnkey partner by phone every month?

Communication was a must for me, and I marked several companies off my list that either did not offer to talk each month or said they did but had poor follow-up and were difficult to reach. I figured if I couldn't talk to them before I purchased when they were trying to sell something to me, it would be impossible to talk with them after I had already bought. In the end, I spoke with other investors and liked that I continually heard that they had good communication.

🔑 Is the person I touch base with at my company the same individual each month?

Yes. I have my own assigned representative at the company who is familiar with me, my family, our situation, and what we expect from communication and our portfolio.

Expanding Your Vision

🔑 What actions am I taking to continue building my portfolio and move closer to my vision?

The biggest actions I take now are reviewing my goals and vision each year. For instance, I have taken several years off in the past from adding to my portfolio when it is performing and meeting my goals. In other years, I have added as many as five properties to my portfolio. Being aware and reviewing years are two actions that have really helped me to build my portfolio.

🔑 Am I continuing to be inspired by my turnkey company to review my portfolio, my goals, and my vision?

Each year I have an appointment with the turnkey companies I work with to review my portfolio and performance. I initiate this conversation so they know I want to see where I stand and see what they think. Since I am so familiar with so many turnkey companies around the country, I also take the time to keep visiting with companies that I have never worked with. This helps me to stay up-to-date with different markets in case I need to make any additional purchases, but it also helps me to hold my turnkey company accountable to giving me the best customer service. Memphis Invest continues to set the bar very high for other companies.

Where is my confidence today as a turnkey real estate investor? What concrete steps can I take to feel even stronger about my investments?

I am very confident that the portfolio I have built will help me reach my goals and achieve my vision. My perfect day is right around the corner! The easiest way to feel stronger as an investor is to connect deeper and more often. Visit the company you have chosen to work with. Spend time with them and meet the team. One visit is great, but visiting on a more routine basis is even better. When you visit, a quick drive-by of your properties is another great way to stay connected and grow in confidence as an investor that you have made a wise choice.

TURNKEY MASTERY TIPS

How long a company has been in business is very important.

A company that came through the real estate market crash and survived shows you that it has good systems and processes in place. A company that started after the crash and was built during the recovery may not have the experience necessary to protect you if and when a market takes a downturn. Keep that in mind!

Creative financing is *not* a good option when you buy turnkey real estate.

If you are not ready financially to invest passively, spend time building your cash. This is not a short-term, quick investment, so do not use creative financing such as money partners, hard money lenders, or borrowing from credit cards. These strategies can work for short-term investments, but not for long-term passive investments such as turnkey.

Follow the steps!

If you are stuck after setting your vision and worried that it may be too big or even not big enough and don't know where to start, follow the steps! Taking the simple action of picking a market to research can be enough to push past your fear and get the ball rolling!

Look for a partner that takes the time to listen and learn.

If you want to build a portfolio of turnkey properties and do it safely, you want to do business with a trustworthy company, right? Right off the bat, pay attention to how urgent the company's people are to get you into buying mode. Pay attention to how quickly they are trying to get you warmed up and writing checks for properties. You want to find a company that is going to be your partner. The best thing your partner can do is go slow and spend some time getting to know you as an investor. There is no way a turnkey company can build a portfolio that fits your needs perfectly if they are not taking time to listen and learn!

Take steady, patient action in the direction of your vision.

Never confuse simply making changes with making progress. Change is not necessarily a sign of making progress.

Cheap properties are not good turnkey investments.

Take a moment and underline the next sentence. Do not buy "cheap" properties! Cheap means less expensive, smaller properties in more impoverished areas of the city. These properties are better left to local, active investors able to put their time into the management and operation of these low-cost, cheap houses. A quality turnkey property will never be priced less than $60,000. Don't be fooled by promises of low prices and high returns. If it sounds easy to make a double-digit return, then don't even consider it for your turnkey portfolio. It is never easy, and quality turnkey investments are not "cheap properties."

Understand the importance of positive cash flow.

There are two ways that real estate investors receive income on a property, but only one that puts dollars in your pocket. Rental income and appreciation are both very important. However, when you start building your portfolio, make sure you are buying properties that will produce a yearly, positive cash flow. Appreciation comes over time, but making a positive cash flow from the beginning is a powerful motivator to keep building.

Don't forget to include your retirement accounts or a retirement account strategy as part of your plan for reaching your vision.

Most real estate investors that I work with build their vision around using their cash and finding a way to leverage into multiple properties. It is only after a little digging on my part that they realize they have an IRA account that they can use as well. A big part of every investor's vision is retirement. How great would it be to own your portfolio inside your IRA and receive the rent payments during retirement tax-deferred or even tax-free?

Make decisions based on facts—*not* feelings.

Just being familiar with a market is not what I consider "digging deep" in your market research. Make sure you don't decide to invest in a market because you are already familiar with it and really like the market. That is not enough. Always do thorough research, and follow the facts!

You do not have to visit a market before you choose to invest.

I get asked quite often if I think visiting markets is important. You do not have to visit a market before you choose to invest. Visiting the market is a step you take to build your rapport with your chosen turnkey partner, and that may happen before or after you have chosen to get started investing, depending upon the circumstances.

If it feels like a sales pitch, it's a sales pitch.

I can't emphasize enough how important it is that whomever you do business with takes the time to get to know you on the front end. Not just what your vision is and how your goals help you get there, but really getting to know if the company is a good fit for you. Pay attention early on to the questions representatives ask and the direction they lead the conversation. If it feels like a sales pitch, then it's a sales pitch.

Avoid Shiny Object Syndrome.

Shiny Object Syndrome is best described as that pit in your stomach that seems to almost always form right after making a big buying decision. It asks if we got the best deal or if we negotiated hard enough. It is the nagging thought that there is always something better than the deal I got or a price lower than the one I am paying. Fight the urge! If you have done your homework and know exactly how an investment fits into your goals and drives you toward your vision, then make the investment.

How do I define value?

I measure the value of my investments by how much money they make relative to how convenient they are for me, and how relatively secure. The return I get has very little to do with the actual value equation I use. It's a reflection of the value I attribute to convenience and security.

Review your plan often to make sure you stay on target.

One of the best tips I can give you is to keep your plan close by and make a habit of reviewing it monthly. For most of you, there will be other investments, savings accounts, or income streams that all play a role in your plan. Keeping an eye on your progress will build your enthusiasm, and celebrating even the small wins will keep you inspired to stay on track.

Celebrate small wins.

"When was the last time I celebrated a small win on the path to my long-term financial goals?" Write this question down as part of your plan. Each time you review your plan you'll be looking for the small wins and making sure you celebrate your steady path toward reaching your goals.

Harness the power of multiple properties.

I always recommend that investors build a portfolio and take advantage of the power of scaling to multiple properties all providing income at the same time. Buying multiple properties lets you take advantage of scale and negotiate better pricing on some of the services if you close more than one property at a time, and having multiple properties lowers risk.

As an investor, you will be on a roller coaster. When your property is occupied and paying you a return, you are 100 percent occupied and happy. When your property is vacant or behind in the rent, you are 100 percent vacant and unhappy. Who needs the aggravation of everything hanging on a single property? If your vision requires you to set a goal of just one property, don't buy turnkey. Figure out another vision with a bigger goal!

Turnkey is great launching pad for future investments.

There are literally thousands of different ways to make money in real estate. Most require a lot of active participation on the part of the investor, but there are also ways to build an active business around passive real estate investing. If you are passionate about real estate and looking for a place to start, turnkey real estate is a great jumping-off point. It allows you to learn many of the ins and outs of real estate while safely building a portfolio. I have worked with many real estate investors who have used their turnkey experience as a launching pad for other real estate investments.

In the end, it's about what's right for you.

Don't make investments just because they look good on paper or based on slick marketing material. Make investments because they fit *your* plan.

You cannot be passive about your passive investments.

There may not be a more important tip in this book. Buying a turnkey property and building your portfolio passively does not mean that you completely abdicate your role to some company in a remote city. It does the heavy lifting, but you still have to keep track of your portfolio's performance. As noted in the Turnkey Safely Checklist questions above, the best way to avoid mistakes is by checking your statements each month and consistently talking with your management company. These are the habits of a successful turnkey investor.

A great partner understands your goals for the long term.

Turnkey is a people business. Your turnkey partner should be a partner in your success. If it is not willing to forgo a few dollars on a deal here or there to make sure you succeed, then keep looking. This is your partner for the lifetime of your portfolio. For some that is going to be a very long time. A great partner is one that understands that your dreams, plans, goals, and vision are all very real things, and is willing to work hand in hand with you to make them come true.

INDEX

ABOUT THE AUTHOR

Chris Clothier is a partner at Memphis Invest, one of the fastest-growing and most well-respected turnkey investment companies in the United States. A successful real estate investor, entrepreneur, speaker, and philanthropist, since 2004 Clothier has helped hundreds of individuals enter and succeed in the world of passive real estate investing. Through Memphis Invest, he, along with his partners, leverage their expertise to bring in over $40 million in rental revenue for their investors annually.

Clothier resides in Memphis, Tennessee, with his wife Michelle and their five children, Grayson, Grant, Sophie, Margo, and Andi Rose. A former professional youth soccer coach, in his spare time, Clothier coaches youth soccer, enjoys attending his children's sporting events, and participates in endurance races.

Chris and Michelle founded Kids Kickin' Cancer Soccer Club in 2017 and fund various charitable organizations including Charity: Water, Pur[SHOE]ing Joy, Caring House Project, and Boston Children's Hospital through their family foundation.

Contact Information
www.ChristopherClothier.com
https://www.facebook.com/christopherclothier/
chris@memphisinvest.com
Chris@ChristopherClothier.com
https://www.linkedin.com/in/chrisdclothier/
https://twitter.com/chrisdclothier

NOTES

NOTES

NOTES

NOTES